(Foreword continued from back flap).

needed. After all, can any education be truly human, that is not truly international? The answer this small study gives is No! And it tells us Why!

GLENN A. OLDS
Executive Dean
International Studies &
World Affairs
State University of New York

International Exchange in Education

THE LIBRARY OF EDUCATION

A Project of The Center for Applied Research in Education, Inc.

G. R. Gottschalk, Director

Categories of Coverage

I	II	III
Curriculum and Teaching	Administration, Organization, and Finance	Psychology for Educators

IV	V	VI
History, Philosophy, and Social Foundations	Professional Skills	Educational Institutions

International Exchange in Education

CUMMINS E. SPEAKMAN, JR.

University of Hawaii

The Center for Applied Research in Education, Inc.
New York

Foreword

Educational innovation rarely comes swiftly. As part of the spirit of the times, it is shaped—silently, often secretly. Fed by many small steps and countless persons, ideas and occasions, the institution of education moves forward slowly. It takes years sometimes to "season" a single idea and even longer to make it a part of the whole culture. In this regard, *internationalizing* education has been a long time coming. The story of that long journey has not been fully or adequately told; its roots are deep, anchored in the cultural diversity of our shrinking planet. Its full meaning and urgent promise is the prophecy of this slender volume.

Dr. Speakman did not set for himself the comprehensive task of covering the wide dimension of his topic. His life has been too full of the crescendo of an idea long delayed which suddenly has come of age for him to spend time and detachment in a scholarly study—though he could. Caught first in the educative task of "internationalizing" German prisoners of war, through distinguished graduate study at Yale University, foreign student advising and teaching at the University of Virginia and at Harvard University, holding an exchange professorship in the Middle East to the task of bringing the curriculum of a college into the last half of the twentieth century at Springfield College where I knew him best, Dr. Speakman brings the authenticity and clarity of this rich background to his writing. He writes with the quiet urgency of one who hears the "running sound of history" in his ears, and with the deep desire to help those too who run to keep up, to take their hearings, find resources, and chart their course in this complex field.

It is appropriate this book should appear in such a distinguished series as the Library of Education Series. The paradox of parochialism in education is heavy upon us, precisely at a time when the world strains toward a common humanity. Even where there are signs of a growing internationalizing in American education, these are often superficial and stage-like: an African in colorful robes at the head

v

table at Homecoming; an elective course such as "Asian Life and Literature" offered in a college catalogue; occasional unrelated "foreign visitors" punctuating the campus with periodic visits.

Dr. Speakman fastens wisely on the "person" as the prime bearer of cultural difference and strings his narrative on that strong thread. He knows that there are human continuities deeper than the eye can see, and that culture is more than clothes deep. He knows, too, that educational reform in this area is long overdue—knows the slow painful process of change as it takes each reluctant step. He writes, therefore, with a fine sense of the need of those who will read the volume—teacher, student, layman, diplomat, and all those engaged in intellectual and cultural exchange. The reader will find an honest narrative, a wise guide, a gentle prophecy. It will not answer all the questions. Books seldom do, but it will stake out the paths we've come along on a long journey, and it will help us find our way forward at a time when international dimensions of education are so clearly needed. After all, can any education be truly human that is not truly international? The answer this small study gives is No! And it tells us Why!

GLENN A. OLDS
Executive Dean
International Studies &
World Affairs
State University of New York

International Exchange in Education

John Dale Russell

One of the remarkable post-war developments in American education has been the great surge of interest and participation in education outside the boundaries of this country. Education has always had its international aspects. Colleges and universities in the United States have long drawn some of their distinguished faculty members from those who have been educated in other countries and students from other countries have been cordially welcomed in American institutions. In the period since World War II, however, at least two important new trends have developed. One is the increasing extent to which personnel of the elementary and secondary schools in the United States—teachers, administrators, pupils—have developed interests in international education. The other is the tremendous increase in the volume of international traffic in institutions of higher education. At some universities, where there is unusually heavy participation in programs of international education, there is current a well-worn witticism, to the effect that, if a faculty meeting is to be called, the attendance will probably be better if the meeting is held in Bangkok or Karachi, than if it is held on the home campus.

Because of limitations of space, Dr. Speakman has not attempted to deal with curriculum in area studies and world affairs. He has concentrated instead on the international exchange of personnel for educational purposes—and, almost exclusively on exchanges in which the United States is involved.

Eminently qualified in background to write on this subject, Dr. Speakman has continued his interest and contribution to international education through his position as Vice President of The Johnson Foundation in Wisconsin. As a part of its work, the Foundation engages in promoting international understanding through conferences on areas and issues. It also provides several fellowships for advanced scholars from abroad.

vii

In the preparation of this monograph, the author has had invaluable assistance from Miss Mary A. Houghton, Program Associate on the staff of the Johnson Foundation. Miss Houghton, who holds a Master's degree from the Johns Hopkins School of Advanced International Studies, has done much of the research, especially the collection and evaluation of bibliographical materials and ably assisted Dr. Speakman at every stage of the book's preparation.

This small volume is intended to be useful to Americans who are thinking about undertaking some educational experience abroad and to citizens of other countries who are thinking about coming to the United States for study, teaching, or research. It abounds with suggestions of sources from which advice and help, including financial help, can be obtained. In short, it is an excellent addition to the Library of Education and a rich reference for anyone contemplating an educational experience abroad.

JOHN DALE RUSSELL
Content Editor

Contents

CHAPTER V

Programs of American Colleges and Universities 75

CHAPTER VI

Conclusion 92

Bibliography 107

Index 113

International Exchange in Education

International education cannot be the work of one country. It is the responsibility and promise of all nations. It calls for free exchange and full collaboration. We expect to receive as much as we give, to learn as well as to teach.

PRESIDENT JOHNSON TO THE CONGRESS OF THE UNITED STATES, FEBRUARY 2, 1966.

CHAPTER I

Educational Exchange in International Relations

The international educational movement has burgeoned in American education since World War II to the point where educational exchange programs are now an inseparable part of the educational system and the nub of cultural diplomacy. With the shrinking of the world and the growth of political interdependence, having a knowledge of the opportunities offered for study, research, and teaching abroad has become increasingly important to Americans. Because of America's specialized know-how along with the emergence of the United States as a world power, desire for knowledge of the opportunities offered for study, research and teaching in the United States has become increasingly important to people of other countries.

The demand to know about international educational opportunities has been met by an overwhelming number of programs and by an almost equally overwhelming flood of studies and publications. This book is not intended to increase the flood. Rather, it is aimed to help students preparing to be elementary or secondary school teachers, or to be on a college faculty, to be school administrators, and all those interested in educational affairs by being a current summary of all the aspects of international educational exchange and by serving as a guide through the maze of literature about opportunities and problems of exchange. Opportunities range from sponsorship by UNESCO to that offered by the Rotary Club of Oshkosh, Wisconsin—with a multitude of government and foundation grants in between. Problems range from inter-cultural conflicts to financially stranded students. This small volume is not a comprehensive listing and examination, but rather an overview—an initial reference for teachers planning careers and for students wanting to study another culture.

Exchanges sponsored by military authorities and missionary organizations were judged to be outside the scope of this book. How-

1

ever, the many exchange programs for persons wanting to receive technical training or wanting to give technical assistance under the auspices of the United States government or under some international agency will be briefly reviewed, since they are significant features of international education.

The book first will take a look at the background of present-day educational exchanges. In earlier years, the values imputed to the exchange of ideas, goods, and people were different from ours but, no one doubts, they were even then viewed as educational. The first cultural contacts were made through military clashes, which bred curiosity and eventually led to an attainment of knowledge about neighboring enemies. Ancient records testify to the fact that there was intermingling and a cross-fertilization of cultures of peoples dwelling in the Tigris and Euphrates valley with those in the Egyptian delta. Since there was proliferation of cultures, the eastern Mediterranean eventually became the crossroads of East-West travel, bringing about an inevitable exchange of ideas.

Next the book will shift attention from an historic review to a discussion of the modern concept of educational exchange. Focus will be on the development, from World War I to the present, of international educational exchange programs in the United States.

Brief descriptions of the types of programs presently offered by national and international institutions, public and private, will be presented. These can serve as prototypes. References will be given to the best sources available for further, more detailed information. It is hoped that, in this way, the book will offer useful guidelines to teachers, students, and administrators about programs best suited to their needs. The bibliography includes key source materials thoughtfully compiled from a voluminous literature.

Finally, the book will make evaluations and analyses of present programs—pointing out the pluses, minuses, and especially the pitfalls. Its aim is not to be exhaustive but to be a guide to the crucial problems and provocative issues involved. This, then, is an effort to help readers test their own thinking and planning against those of persons who have already been a part of the exchange program and have become professionals in the field of international education as a result of their experiences.

The international educational exchange movement in the United States is a unique blending of several peculiarly American characteristics. Typically American, the movement depends on both private initiative and financing and on government coordination and support. A remarkable agency, the Institute of International Education, has evolved to administer the program. Here is a private organization administering government programs, sometimes sending foreigners financed by public and private funds to state and private campuses. With the impetus of federal legislation, two thousand institutions of higher education in the United States have come up with what sometimes seems like twenty thousand programs. Another anomaly is the lopsided character of what educators call exchange of persons. The proportion of foreign students, teachers, administrators, and scholars in the United States to those abroad from the United States probably is more than 4 to 1.[1]

There is no doubt that international educational exchange has been wholeheartedly accepted in the United States. It offers a contemporary interpretation of the command "love thy neighbor." In another peculiarly American combination, international educational exchange has appeal to two strands of American political philosophy —pragmatism and idealism. To the pragmatist good cultural relations helps business flourish and promotes peace. The businessman has a stake in preserving the latter since peace *is* profitable. Thus American businessmen approve of using cultural means to advance economic ends.

At the same time, idealists approve of using cultural means to further political ends. Such non-political cooperation, particularly to the functionalist school of thought, is a means to an end—that of eventually securing political cooperation. Some American idealists hold the optimistic faith that person-to-person contacts, first-hand looks at political and economic institutions in the United States, and confrontation with the lovable personalities of American people will bring international understanding and peace. Realism sometimes intrudes on both of these idealistic visions so that the approach backfires. Nevertheless, both the idealistic and the pragmatic attitudes make international educational exchange congenitally agreeable to the American people.

---

[1] Institute of International Education, *Open Doors 1965* (New York: The Institute, 1965), pp. 4–13.

Cultural Exchange Begins with Envoys

In the dawning days of man's slow rise to civilization, the earliest communication between cultures undoubtedly was the hostile clash that took place between neighboring groups while protecting their territories at the boundary line. Here even whole cultures were participants in "the survival of the fittest," as one culture conquered another and established its reign. C. Northcote Parkinson terms this "cultural inundation" and praises its results:

> It is a commonplace among students of history that the brightest inventions (like the alphabet) can be traced very often to the borderlands between one culture and another . . . People of disputed provinces have been presented with alternating sets of ideas and are compelled finally to form a synthesis or make a choice. After many unhappy experiences—campaigns and massacres, dissensions and disputes—they become more mentally alert and agile than people whose lives have been less disturbed.[2]

Parkinson describes two stages in this contact. The first wave of contact was primarily of missionaires, traders, and teachers; the second wave of the administrators.[3] This process is the main concern of this chapter: the first and second waves of contact that prepared the way for the present-day phenomenon of an international educational exchange of persons.

Following the first, probably unfriendly, contacts between neighboring groups, a formal system for handling relations on a friendly basis developed. (Harold Nicholson suggests that the diplomatic method originated when the anthropoid apes, inhabiting one group of caves, saw the profit of reaching an understanding with those in another area regarding the limits of hunting territory.) Negotiations were impossible unless the emissaries had diplomatic immunity.[4] Granting immunity to the other's envoy guaranteed the immunity of one's own envoy and, with that peaceful contact between neighbors, the history of peaceful cultural interchange begins.

As with so many of the earliest examples of human institutions, the Sumerian civilization gives one of the first evidences of the insti-

---

[2] C. Northcote Parkinson, *East and West* (Boston: Houghton Mifflin Company, 1963), p. 95.

[3] *Ibid.,* pp. xi–xxii.

[4] Harold Nicholson, *The Evolution of Diplomatic Method* (London: Constable and Co., Ltd., 1954), p. 2.

tution of diplomacy. A famous Sumerian epic tells of a "battle of wills" that took place between two Sumerian city-states. It was conducted by sending a herald back and forth with increasingly menacing messages. In Egypt, the famous tablets at Tel-el-Amarna show that during the reign of Amenhotep III in the fourteenth century B.C., the kings of the Hittites, of Cyprus, Mitanni, Assyria, and Babylonia corresponded and exchanged presents with Amenhotep. About 1000 B.C. ambassadors of the Hittite king were granted plenipotentiary powers to settle disputes.

Although we know that the "vanquished" were sometimes brought to the kingdom of their conquerors for education in the ancient Egypt of Amenhotep's father, or were brought as hostages in the Roman empire (to guarantee obedience to treaties), there is little evidence of diplomacy directly serving educational or even cultural purposes until the rise of imperialism in the nineteenth century. But throughout the historical period, the diplomatic method was evolving as cultural contacts were made easier by establishing formal channels to handle them.

The early diplomatic voyages of Menelaus and Odysseus to Troy to save Helen, and of Ajax, Odysseus, and Phoenix to appease Achilles were more formally prescribed by custom than is usually realized. Later, although developing the administration and the rule of peoples of differing cultures to a high level, the Romans did little to embellish the Greek art of diplomacy. The Byzantine Emperors introduced the custom of a special department to deal with relations with foreign governments and initiated the training of professional negotiators, while the Italians established the first permanent resident embassy in a foreign country.[5]

In eighteenth century Europe when loyalty was less swayed by nationalism than it is today, diplomatists and intellectuals and students attached themselves to foreign courts and schools more randomly. Nevertheless, they carried a cultural heritage and were the *modus vivendi* of intercultural communication in Europe. Voltaire serves as the prototype of these eighteenth and nineteenth century cosmopolitans. He lived at both the English and Prussian courts, enticed by the patronage of Queen Caroline of England and also by Frederick the Great of Prussia. During each sojourn he published

---

[5] *Ibid.*, pp. 3–33.

some of his writings in the host country. He both learned from and taught the foreign country in which he resided.

It was the nineteenth century imperialistic impulse which directly related the diplomatic contact with cultural aspects, causing governments to initiate planned programs of educational activities having an international dimension. Diplomacy relied on personal relationships among an elite group in the nineteenth century. The brand of nearly intra-cultural communication which marked the Congress of Vienna prevailed during many of the years of peace that followed. "The White Man's Burden" of the British, the *mission civilisatrice* of the French, the *Kultur* of the Germans were the rationalizations of imperialism's educational aspect. The British Council and the French cultural attaché were the first institutions established to handle cultural relations with the other civilizations of the world. The colonization of the non-Western world included exportation of the mother country's educational systems to the colonies, sometimes to the point of identical replications.

The tradition of a cosmopolitan education sometimes combined with this imperialistic impulse and produced unique, intelligent, sensitive men whose educations were cosmopolitan and whose careers were international. They made an extraordinary contribution to the cultural relations between their government and that of the countries they travelled in. The comments of T. E. Lawrence in his introduction to the Englishman Charles Doughty's *Travels in Arabia Deserta* serve as witness to this:

> I have found that he had become history in the desert . . . They tell tales of him, making something of a legend of the tall and impressive figure, very wise and gentle, who came to them like a herald of the outside world . . . He was the first Englishman they had met. He predisposed them to give a chance to other men of his race because they found him honorable and good.[6]

Lawrence, himself, had already become an extraordinary cultural link and a legendary figure in Arabia when he wrote this.

Some of this group became the empire's leading diplomats and top administrators. In the middle of the nineteenth century the French physician, consul in Mosul, Paul Emile Botta, investigated the strange mounds outside Mosul. This led to the first discovery of

---

[6] Charles M. Doughty, *Travels in Arabia Deserta* (London: Jonathan Cape, 1936), p. 19.

the Assyrian culture which had been lost for 2500 years. Austen Layard was a second and even more famous example of a cultured and educated European whose intelligence and sensitivity yielded an outstanding cultural contribution. Educated in Italy and England, master of Persian and other languages, he rode into Mosul in 1839, a vagabond. After acquiring funds from Sir Stratford Canning, he discovered the famous mound of Nimrud with the palace of Assurnasipal II and, at the nearby mound of Kuyunjik, the palace of Sennacherib. These fantastic discoveries of the Assyrian civilization were exhibited in 1854 at the London Crystal Palace when Layard was British Undersecretary for Foreign Affairs.

In a different vein, such English travelers as Lady Hester Stanhope and Sir Charles Burton were assimilated by the foreign lands they visited. Lady Hester quit England at the death of her uncle, William Pitt; she travelled extensively in the Middle East, and eventually settled among the half-savage tribes near Mount Lebanon, gaining the reputation among them of a prophetess. Sir Charles Burton joined the East India Company. After becoming a linguist and expert in Indian affairs, he made a successful pilgrimage to Mecca disguised as an Indian Pathan. Later, he travelled to Somali, searched for the source of the Nile, entered the British foreign service, and was a consul in Brazil, Damascus, and Trieste.

There were Americans venturing about the world, on a smaller scale than the Europeans but accomplishing similar ends. A long history elapsed between Pocahantas' visit to the English court and the sending of distinguished Americans to represent the United States government abroad. America's early representatives were ofttimes intellectuals of great repute—Benjamin Franklin, Washington Irving, Nathaniel Hawthorne, William Dean Howells, James Russell Lowell—forerunners of today's visiting scholars.

These cultural contacts, made within a diplomatic framework, began with a trickle of official envoys and gathered momentum in the cosmopolitan and imperial nineteenth century until it culminated in the massive programs of the twentieth century educational exchange.

The Early International Educational Centers
and Visiting Scholars

The forebears of today's educational exchange programs are the wandering scholars and the international centers of learning to which they gravitated. From the moment that individuals in one culture spoke to individuals in another culture, the process of exchanging ideas was underway. Very quickly the exchange of ideas incidental to military and diplomatic contacts was supplanted by purposely planned intellectual exchanges. The Sumerians again furnish an early example—a literary borrowing which is one of the most ancient of written scholarly exchanges. The Semitic *Epic of Gilgamesh* contains sections dating from the seventeenth and eighteenth centuries B.C. which had been borrowed from ancient Sumerian poems.

The city of Alexandria was one of the first international centers of learning. The Library and Museum, established there in 332 B.C. by Ptolemy and a peripatetic scholar and statesman named Demetrius of Phalerum, attracted students from Europe, Asia Minor, and North Africa. The museum was a center for the advancement of science; by 150 A.D. the library had 700,000 volumes. Later the magnetism of cultural Athens surpassed Alexandria as contact increased between Rome and Athens. Many Romans, including Antonius, Cicero, Brutus, and Horace, went to study at Athens, as it became the university center of the world. The Sophists in Athens were proud of the cosmopolitan nature of their student body. One of the Sophists, Libanius, in the fourth century A.D. was, however, "too modest" to claim that he "filled the three continents and all of the islands with rhetoricians."[7] The Greek intellectual centers, from the fourth century B.C. to the fourth century A.D., exerted a powerful attraction on the scholars of the ancient world. The ancient Greek models continue to influence modern education: the Doctor of Philosophy degree still emulates the Greek elevation of philosophy and modern education still assembles experts and students from all over the world at great university centers.

As the Hellenic period dominated by the Roman imperium advanced, other university centers were established. By the time of

---

[7] John W. H. Walden, *The Universities of Ancient Greece* (New York: Charles Scribner's Sons, 1909), p. x.

Justinian, the school of Roman law was flourishing in Beirut, a city which is still an international academic center, due to the presence of the French St. Joseph University and the American University of Beirut. The latter began as the Protestant Syrian college in Damascus in 1866 and in 1966 is a university with a student population of over 3,000, drawn from throughout the Middle East and the rest of the world.

Just as the conquests of Alexander brought an exchange of ideas between the Persian and Greek civilizations and the ultimate Hellenization of the empire, so the *jihad,* or holy wars, prescribed by Mohammed brought the Arabisation of many lands and the exchange of ideas between the Islamic and Christian civilizations. The influence of the Arab conquests on education in the West was such that according to Alvaro, a Christian from Cordova, ". . . Among thousands of us there is hardly one who can write a passable Latin letter to a friend but innumerable are those who can express themselves in Arabic and compose poetry in that language with greater art than the Arabs themselves."[8] The wave of Arab traders who followed the Arab conquerors contributed to the important transmission of Greek philosophy to the West (through the transmission of the Arabian commentaries on Aristotle and Plato made by Avicenna and Averroes to the scholars in Spain and Sicily).

In eastern Asia, too, scholars and scholarly works were travelling long distances for knowledge's sake. Chinese, Japanese, and Korean scholars studied Buddhism at the great ancient Indian universities and translated Buddhist scriptures and books into Chinese. Indian scholars journeyed to China and did similar translations into Chinese there. Contacts between the Far East and Western Europe were made by educated men such as Marco Polo, who taught Western religion, arts and customs to the Kublai Khan. Marco Polo travelled through the Chinese provinces in the thirteenth century at the Khan's request. Matteo Ricci, an Italian Jesuit of the sixteenth century, steeped himself in Chinese culture, produced many Chinese scholarly works, and won favor by teaching Western inventions to the Chinese.

In the Middle Ages in Europe, it was the Church, heir to Rome, that became the repository of knowledge of the ancient world and

---

[8] Bernard Lewis, *The Arabs in History* (New York: Harper Torchbooks, 1960), p. 123.

which served as the vehicle of cultural and intellectual interchange. Scholarly churchmen founded medieval schools and universities; as they travelled over Europe, they served as the exchange scholars of that period. An example: St. Columba (Columbanus 543–615) an Irish missionary who built the abbey of Luxeuil in France later moved to Switzerland (610) where he preached to the Alemanni. He died in Italy where he had founded the monastery of Bobbio. St. Columba was a writer, a poet, a man of learning acquainted with the Latin and Greek classics.

There are many other examples of the cultural exchange of the *Moyen age,* but it remained for the movement known as "The Crusades" to bring about cultural interchange on a large scale. Men of all the European nations, first impelled by Pope Urban II's imperative, *Dieu le vult!* (God wills it)—or by curiosity, desire for adventure or a hundred other reasons—drew together in polyglot armies, marched across Europe with the intention of wresting the Holy Sepulchre from the Infidel and of establishing a Christian kingdom in the East. Thousands perished along the way. Though the period of Christian control of the Holy Land lasted less than a century, the effects upon the peoples of Europe and the peoples of the East were incalculable in terms of exchange of ideas, customs, scientific knowledge, goods, and language. Arabic knowledge was transmitted to Europe along with spices, fabrics, drugs, perfumes. There was a vast interchange of literature: stories, legends, and "things of the imagination." Songs and epics of heroic deeds of European knights and Saracen kings were a part of this interchange. The intermingling of the Europeans themselves, serving together in a common cause, was equally important in this intercultural exchange.

In the same period, the Norman Conquest of England provided impetus for a revival of learning in England. This came about with the introduction of the ecclesiastical system of bishops and abbots who received their training in excellent centers of Norman letters, notably at Bec and Caen.[9]

English savants commonly pursued their scholarly preparation abroad. Alfred of Sareschal (Anglicus), an outstanding lecturer in science at Oxford in the 11th century, is but one example. He received his first training in Aristotelian thought under Saloman Aven-

---

[9] Sister Mary Justine, O.S.F., *Learning in England in the Twelfth Century* (unpublished manuscript, Cardinal Stritch College, Milwaukee, Wisconsin, 1955), p. 2.

roza in Toledo. While in Spain, he translated from the Arabic the pseudo-Aristotelian works (*De Vegetabilis*) (*De Plantis*) and parts of the *Meterology* of Avicenna.[10]

With the development of the great medieval universities at Bologna and Paris, the great Greek universities found worthy heirs. The many foreign scholars grouped themselves into "nations," a term for protective associations with a geographical connotation vaguer than today's. The very word "universitatis," base of the English "university," was originally given only to institutions whose students came from a variety of geographical regions. The international composition of the student body and faculty combined with a nearly unanimous adherence to Aristotelian philosophy produced schools materially and intellectually international.

Later generations developed intellectual propositions to institutionalize this theologically-based medieval internationalism in a secular framework. John Amos Comenius, a Czech bishop of the enlightenment, advocated the establishment of a Pansophic College for scholars of all nations in order to coordinate knowledge for international understanding. Vattel, father of international law, in *Le Droit des Gens,* states that the exchange of teachers is a common duty, a service to humanity which nations should render to each other. Later Marc Antoine Jullien suggested that a specific commission of education be established to collect and disseminate information on European education.[11]

Eased by prosperity, peace, and imperial rule in nineteenth century Europe, the custom of journeying to distant and prestigious centers of learning proliferated. Descendants of the great medieval universities, the great nineteenth century German, French and English Universities became Meccas for students, both Western and non-Western, seeking the best education. German universities, most popular of all, enrolled 477 foreign students in 1835 and 3,097 in 1904.[12]

The student missions from non-Western civilizations were an in-

---

[10] *Ibid.,* p. 18.

[11] William W. Brickman, "International Education" in *Encyclopedia of Educational Research,* Walter S. Monroe, ed. (New York: The Macmillan Company, 1950), p. 618.

[12] Spencer Stoker, *Schools and International Understanding* (Chapel Hill, N.C.: The University of North Carolina Press, 1933), p. xxi.

herently interesting phenomenon. These were forerunners of a significant portion of the contemporary traffic of the international educational exchange movement. The writings of Tahatawi, a brilliant Egyptian student sent to France as part of the student missions of Mohammed Ali, testify to the impact of Western culture on these students; his was the most important book in Egypt for a century. Sent mainly to learn military science, these non-Western students unavoidably encountered Western philosophy, literature, and general education. They returned home with revelations enabling them to open the door for modernizing their countries. Such students continue to come, perhaps for different motives, but with similar results.

The nineteenth century also saw the organization of international educational institutions. Between 1851 and 1915 seventeen international educational congresses were held. In 1895 the first international federation of students was formed; in 1905 the first international federation of teachers and in 1912 of secondary teachers.[13]

The technological revolution of the twentieth century revolutionized the methods of intercultural contact briefly discussed here. Modern military methods meant more people were involved in warfare; modern communication meant more people were alert about diplomatic relations among nations; modern transportation meant more people could travel to more places in search of education. The breakdown of these areas, traditionally belonging to the elite, changed the role of the average man in the world and made possible the present phenomenon of international educational exchange and cultural diplomacy.

International Exchange from the Nineteenth Century to the Second World War

The travelling students of the nineteenth century were frequently the children of the well-to-do who went abroad because they felt obtaining a foreign degree highly prestigious. Although sometimes they might have brought their experiences back to an academic or scientific community, they were not the forerunners of the current generation of trans-oceanic student travellers having a significant influence in both their native and host countries. It was the advances made in transportation and communication in the late nineteenth

---

13 *Ibid.,* pp. xviii–xxi.

and early twentieth centuries which shrivelled the world and from which an international perspective developed, leading to the *institutionalization* of international education. This section of the book focuses on the development of the first institutions and programs for international educational exchange available to the general public.

In 1840 the United States provided for its first official relations of a cultural nature—a joint resolution of Congress approved the exchange of published materials between the Library of Congress and foreign libraries. In 1867 the Smithsonian Institution became responsible for the interchange of documents to and from abroad. In 1867 the first annual report of the United States Commissioner of Education contained information on foreign education. But not until some twenty years later were studies of foreign education undertaken by the "Bureau of Education." About that time, the National Bureau of Standards became the official host to visiting foreign scientists and technicians.[14]

Although 1,300 Cuban teachers came to Harvard in 1900 via army transports for a summer of English and other courses,[15] international scholarships were unknown until the twentieth century. The Rhodes fund, set up in 1902 to promote understanding between England and Germany and the United States through the exchange of students, was the first significant effort in that direction.

In 1909 the Association for the International Interchange of Students was established for students from Great Britain, Canada, and the United States. In 1911 the American Scandinavian Foundation received half a million dollars to be used partially for student exchanges, offering six scholarships each year.

Shortly thereafter, several unique arrangements were made for the exchange of groups of students which foreshadow the historic permission to use accumulated foreign currencies for education of the Fulbright Amendment of 1946. In 1909, Theodore Roosevelt suggested, in a stroke of diplomatic genius, the use of a portion of the Boxer Indemnity fund to send Chinese students to the United States for further education. As a result, eighteen million dollars were spent for the education of 2,000 Chinese students in American colleges and universities.[16] Another such mobilization of funds oc-

---

[14] Charles A. Thomson and Walter H. C. Laves, *Cultural Relations and United States Foreign Policy* (Bloomington: Indiana University Press, 1963), p. 29.

[15] *Ibid.*

[16] *Ibid.*

curred in 1920 when the establishment of the Belgian American Foundation resulted after the liquidation of the Belgian Relief Commission. During the next twenty-five years, 700 Belgian and American students were exchanged, and, in 1939, alumni of this program held one-fourth of the university teaching positions in Belgium. The alumni also had provided Belgium with a prime minister and six cabinet members. In 1923 Herbert Hoover, as Secretary of Commerce, tried to divert war debts to educational purposes but he failed.[17] Three decades later, in 1951, Congress approved the use of the Finnish war debt payments for exchange programs between Finland and the United States.

Although scholarly exchange with Europe ceased during World War I, the war itself spawned (in its aftermath) a broader interest in other cultures.[18] The Versailles Conference at the end of the war exemplifies international cross-cultural relations. Woodrow Wilson, the first American President to travel abroad, attended the conference for reasons not unlike those popularly rationalized by advocates of educational exchange programs. He wanted to meet the leaders of the Big Four person-to-person in order to be most effective and, seemingly, to teach them by manifesting the principles of democratic government. Gaston Bouthol has explained that Wilson was defeated at Versailles and in Congress because his ideas were "one war too soon."[19] It was also "just one war too soon" for a system of cultural relations which an effective League of Nations might have provided; only since World War II have international organizations provided such services.

The maimed League of Nations did establish a Committee on Intellectual Cooperation, under the chairmanship of Henri Bergson. Its distinguished members recommended exchanges of students and teachers; they sponsored studies and handbooks whose very titles are forerunners of those in this field today.[20] Europeans established

---

[17] *Ibid.,* p. 61.

[18] The French government did allow qualified men in the United States armed services to enter French universities after the armistice and before their return to the United States.

[19] Gaston Bouthol, *On War,* Sylvia and George Lessom, trans. (New York: Walker and Company, 1963).

[20] International Institute on Intellectual Cooperation, *Handbook of National Centers of Educational Information* (Paris, 1934); and *University Exchanges in Europe* (Paris, 1928).

the International Folk High School in Elsinore, Denmark in 1921; the *Institut Universitaire de Hautes Etudes Internationales* in Geneva in 1927; and the *Deutsche Padagogische Auslandsstelle* in 1929. Although assisted by the establishment of the International Institute of Intellectual Cooperation in Paris, a limited budget and a lack of organization prevented the Bergson Committee from having more than limited influence.[21]

During the inter-war period, a number of new private international organizations and universities were founded which further institutionalized international education: in the United States the Institute of International Education was established in 1919; the International Institute of Columbia University's Teachers College was founded in 1923; abroad the *Bureau International d'Education* of the *Institut Jean Jacques Rousseau* was organized in Geneva in 1929 to disseminate information on education and to organize educational research. The *Bureau* had inter-governmental status.[21]

In the United States, governmental response to these moves was slight. Although the United States had signed the Nine Power Treaty, the Washington Naval Treaty, and the London Treaty, as well as the Kellogg-Briand Pact of Paris, and had agreed to the Dawes and Young Plans for the reconstruction of Europe, these were, by and large, merely formal (even insubstantial) commitments to world affairs. As such, they allowed the United States to become increasingly isolationist—until its entry into World War II. Even though government reactions tended toward isolationism, there was an increase in the international flow of people. During the 1930's, American missionaries, businessmen, English language teachers, scientists, scholars and artists, tourists and journalists crisscrossed the Atlantic. Means of quicker transportation and communication, the multiplication of international congresses all helped facilitate professional and personal friendships between peoples of different countries.

Much of this sort of communication was supported and stimulated by philanthropic foundations. A long history of private philanthropy preceded World War I. Andrew Carnegie's support of scientific projects benefited many lands. The World Peace Foundation established in 1910 by Edward Ginn and the Carnegie Endowment for Interna-

---

21 Brickman, *op. cit.,* p. 620.

tional Peace established the same year lent tremendous support to the efforts of the internationalists.[22] It was during the inter-war years that the efforts of American philanthropy to deepen international understanding grew markedly. The Carnegie Endowment supported (1) aid for libraries abroad, (2) the publication of a history of World War I by foreign scholars under the direction of James Shotwell, and (3) programs for the improvement of education in Africa. The Rockefeller Foundation involved itself on the international level (1) by sponsoring research in health, (2) by supporting foreign affairs organizations, (3) by promoting Latin American studies. The Institute of Pacific Relations promoted better East-West understanding. Between World War I and 1934 the Rockefeller Foundation had spent $15 million on the exchange of scholars.[23]

Another philanthropic program was developed by the Commonwealth Fund which in 1924 provided twenty (and later thirty) fellowships for graduates of British universities to use as a two-year study in the United States.

World War II and International Exchange

More than any previous war in history, World War II mixed peoples, bred curiosity about others, and developed the feeling of "one world." The Department of State and the Office of War Information programmed educational and cultural exchange and established information programs on an international level. In addition, the branches of the armed services found that they had to meet the war situation by producing *experts* on foreign affairs. Such selected personnel had to be trained. Schools, such as the School of Military Government at the University of Virginia and the Navy's special schools for intensive language training, were established to meet this demand.

A similar cross-cultural education occurred conversely—in the Allied prisoner-of-war camps. "Intellectual diversion" programs were devised under the authority of the Secretary of State, Secretary of War, and the Provost-Marshal General. These were special re-education courses in American history, in political science, and in

---

[22] Merle Curti, *American Philanthropy Abroad: A History* (New Brunswick, N.J.: Rutgers University Press, 1963), pp. 197–198.

[23] *Ibid.*, pp. 303–316.

English language training. A large number of the 350,000 German prisoners-of-war in the United States were thus exposed to American culture and *mores* and they carried this experience back to Germany with them. In some camps, prisoners even worked for credit in their native universities through correspondence courses. Upon release, many of these sought a university education in post-war Germany and later became teachers. Quite a few former prisoners came to the United States on exchange programs in the 1940's and 1950's.

After the war the immediate need was for reconstruction of the devastated countries and for the re-education of totalitarian populations. Aid to education was given through the Marshall Plan. The technicians who were sent abroad through the "Point Four" program were among the first to travel abroad to give technical assistance. Under the Occupied Areas Programs, the Army began bringing nationals to the United States—from Germany and Austria in 1947 and from Japan and the Ryukyu islands in 1949—and sent American specialists to those areas. By the end of 1952, 6,000 Germans had visited the United States.[24]

The tragedy of war led to another type of cross-cultural education. As refugees crossed national boundaries to enter crowded camps and later to settle in adopted homelands, they learned about a new culture and, in turn, taught their new compatriots about an old one. The mass movement of the homeless continued and was enlarged with the partition of Palestine in the Arab-Israeli conflict, and by the Korean war, and the other so-called "little wars" of the past decade. Among the refugees have been many prominent scholars, scientists, and professors whose contributions to the countries to which they immigrated are incalculable. The most prominent scientists in United States atomic and nuclear development, and the many scholars in the social sciences need only to be mentioned to illustrate this.

Post-war United States government suddenly found it needed reliable advice about its many new foreign commitments which meant it needed personnel versed in the culture and needs of many heretofore ignored geographical areas. Response to these new pressures led to the development of some of the early schools of international

---

24 Committee on Educational Interchange Policy, *Twenty Years of United States Government Programs in Cultural Relations* (New York: Institute of International Education, 19—), pp. 6–7.

affairs. The Woodrow Wilson School of Foreign Affairs grew out of the School of Military Government at the University of Virginia; the School of Advanced International Studies in Washington appeared in response to the expression of this need on the part of some government officials; and the Foreign Service Institute of the Department of State was developed in response to the new demands on the Foreign Service. As more and more American students desire to learn more about foreign areas, and, as the need for trained personnel has grown with the increasing involvement of the United States in world affairs, the number of international programs has grown. The recent National Defense Education Act has offered additional financial support in this area.

Many of those who actually fought in the wars—the veterans themselves, influenced by their overseas experience—also wanted to enroll in such educational programs. The GI Bill was passed to provide financial support to these veterans. Some veterans made return trips to areas in which they had served and to other foreign lands that interested them. Here again, the foundations and the government provided financial support. Since the war, many who served in the armed services overseas have become teachers in secondary schools and in colleges. Their personal experiences are no doubt still filtering through to the generation of students who are now exploring and studying in today's cultural metropoles and outposts.

Underlying the government's need for trained personnel and students' desire for knowledge about and experience in lands overseas is the widespread belief, ironically re-vitalized by war, that war could be avoided in the future if only people learn more about each other. Some political scientists contend that cooperation on non-political levels will lead to political cooperation and thus lessen the chance of war; the average citizen holds a prevalent belief that if foreigners could only see what we are really like, they would not fight with us. H. Bradford Westerfield aptly states this belief: "the best way to convey an idea is to embody it in a human being and send him to the place where the idea should be implanted."[25] This is the "people-to-people" concept. Along with this concept is a renaissance of American faith in education—this time in international education. Thus, the American people through their government and their edu-

---

[25] H. Bradford Westerfield, *The Instruments of American Foreign Policy* (New York: Thomas E. Crowell Company, 1963), p. 245.

cational institutions have provided their children with opportunities to learn about the world first-hand.

It must be remembered that the institutionalizing of international education is not by its very nature an American phenomenon. Rather, international educational exchange is an integral part of *international* organization, and each depends upon the other for its very existence.

CHAPTER II

International Organizations and International Exchange

The belief, prevalent after World War II, that improved international understanding would prevent another global war was accompanied by the corollary that a peaceful world was best approached by cooperation on non-political levels until:

> a network of such organizations could be created which would absorb, one by one, successive fields of international activity and might even end, like the Lilliputians, in tying down the Gulliver of politics while he slept . . .[1]

Whether the many new international organizations created after World War II were a response to this theory of the school of political scientists termed functionalist, or to some less rational human urge, there was a proliferation of international organizations, many of which developed programs for educational exchange during the next two decades. In fact, their technical assistance, educational exchanges, and seminar-center projects are among the most concrete and potentially valuable contributions these international organizations, often bogged down in bureaucracy and verbosity, have made.

The United Nations (UN)

The Charter of the United Nations, written at the San Francisco Conference in April, 1945, contains several direct references to the objectives of international cultural cooperation and educational exchange. Article 1 lists among its objectives "to achieve international cooperation in solving international problems of an economic, social, cultural, or humanitarian character." Article 13 lists as one of the functions of the General Assembly "the General Assembly shall initiate and make recommendations for the purpose of promoting international cooperation in the economic, social, cultural, educa-

---

[1] H. G. Nicholas, *The United Nations as a Political Institution* (London: Oxford University Press, 1959), p. 6.

20

tional, and health fields." Article 55 states that one of the organization's main functions is "to promote international and educational cooperation." Among the duties of the Economic and Social Council is "to make or initiate studies and reports with respect to international economic, social, cultural, educational and health fields" according to Article 62. At the least, the Charter of the United Nations was implicit with promises of international educational exchange.

These ideas became more explicit and concrete as the educational exchange programs developed and moved forward rapidly, under the special agencies of the United Nations. These programs furthered the philosophy of international organization as a peacekeeping mechanism by opening many avenues of cooperation. And among its immediate post-war tasks was the United Nations' responsibility for the well-being (and education) of refugees, prisoners-of-war, and residents of trusteeship territories. Evolving from this early responsibility is its current role of administering many programs of technical assistance to nationals in newly-independent states.

In practice, the administration of international educational exchange programs under the auspices of the United Nations has devolved upon the Economic and Social Council, its regional commissions, and the various specialized agencies of the United Nations. Information about these programs can be found most readily in the publication of the United Nations Economic Social and Cultural Organization (UNESCO) entitled *Study Abroad*.[2] Beginning with the 1964 edition, it contains information about the programs for educational grants to the United Nations and its agencies, of intergovernmental international organizations such as the Organization of American States, and of non-governmental (i.e. private) international organizations. In addition, there is a comprehensive listing of every country's programs of educational exchange. Each listing contains information about the headquarters, type of study, number of positions open, duration of grant or program, amount of support, qualifications required and procedure of application. In 1964, 130,000 separate opportunities were listed.

---

[2] United Nations Educational Social and Cultural Organization, *Study Abroad, An International Directory of Fellowships, Scholarships and Awards, 1964–1966,* Paris, 1964. Some information previously found in this publication and in other UNESCO publications is now found in the new UNESCO publication, *Handbook of International Exchanges.*

The Economic and Social Council and its regional commissions. The Economic and Social Council supervises the many technical assistance programs of the United Nations. Its Bureau of Technical Assistance Operations Fellowships administers training programs in social welfare, demography, public administration, and other fields, which are open to nationals of all member states, but particularly to those who are or will be holding important positions in developing countries. The regional commissions of the Economic and Social Council concentrate on the affairs of a specific geographical area. They have established a number of regional centers for training programs for individuals from member countries inside, and sometimes outside, the geographical area. Thus economists and statisticians from Bulgaria, Cyprus, Malta, Poland, and Rumania have attended in-service training programs sponsored by the Economic Commission for Europe (ECE). Latin Americans from nineteen countries have attended annual Latin American Institutes for Economic and Social Planning in Santiago, Chile, which were sponsored by the Economic Commission for Latin America (ECLA). Asian nationals are enrolled in training courses at centers at Lahore in Pakistan, New Delhi in India, and Rangoon in Burma, which are under the auspices of the Economic Commission for Asia and the Far East (ECAFE).

In addition, the United Nations organization offers summer internships to foreign students studying in Canada and the United States; financial support to students from trust territories and non-self-governing territories for post-primary technical and university training; and a training program at its New York headquarters for young diplomats from new nations.

The United Nations Educational, Social and Cultural Organization (UNESCO). UNESCO is the agency of the United Nations specifically charged to foster peace by encouraging educational and cultural cooperation. Its predecessor was the International Institute of Intellectual Cooperation of the League of Nations. The Ministers of Education of war-torn countries began to plan for the restoration of education during the war; they convened in London in November, 1945 and drew up the plans for UNESCO. Although its methods of operation are frequently criticized, it remains the major international administrative body for international educational exchange.

Among the many diverse activities of UNESCO are:

1. Publication of handbooks such as the invaluable *Study Abroad* and the *Handbook of International Exchanges.*

2. The convening of many international conferences on international cultural relations and education.

3. Grants for education abroad—to educational administrators, technical and vocational school teachers, female educational leaders, university faculty members in Africa and Latin America, students of finance and statistics.

4. Study tours of a shorter duration for workers, students, and leaders of teacher organizations.

5. Travel grants for youth movement workers and leaders.

6. Maintenance of a center near Paris for briefings of international experts travelling abroad.

7. An International Exchanges Service which administers several thousand fellowships (including some which it has not financed).

Applicants usually apply to the appropriate ministry of their country. United States citizens may apply to the Management Staffing Officer of the International Recruitment Service of the Department of State or to the Technical Assistance Bureau of the Office of Education of the Department of Health, Education, and Welfare.

The other specialized agencies.   The other specialized agencies of the United Nations[3] also have programs of grants for educational exchange and for the support of technical training programs and centers. Again here, *Study Abroad* is the most convenient and comprehensive guide. Although these programs are directed primarily toward the nationals of developing countries, there are oftentimes opportunities for students, teachers, and scholars from the advanced nations to get further technical and professional training in another country.

For example, the World Health Organization offers fellowships for individual study as well as group training programs, lasting from six to twelve months, to approximately 1,500 persons each year. It sends professors to other countries. The International Labor Organization, the only agency dating from the days of the League of Na-

---

[3] These include the International Monetary Fund; the International Bank for Reconstruction and Development; the Food and Agriculture Organization; the World Health Organization; the International Atomic Energy Commission; the International Telegraph Union; and the Universal Postal Union.

tions, offers fellowships and administers training centers for students from developing countries—for advanced technical and vocational training in Turin, Italy, and for labor studies in Geneva. Application to these programs of specialized agencies of the United Nations should be made to the appropriate ministries of the applicant's country.

Inter-governmental Organizations

Another phenomenon of post-war politics, regional alliances and inter-governmental organizations, has spawned a number of opportunities for international educational exchange. Those major organizations to which the United States belongs are the North Atlantic Treaty Organization (NATO) the South East Asia Treaty Organization (SEATO) and the Organization of American States (OAS). Some of the inter-governmental organizations have programs open to nationals of non-member countries. *Study Abroad* is the best reference for information about these programs. It should be noted that the exchange programs of these organizations, with the exception of the Organization of American States, are frequently limited to a rather small number of participants.

The North Atlantic Treaty Organization (NATO) program offers fellowships of two to six months' duration to experienced individuals possessing the Ph.D. degree for studies which will lead to publications on topics of common interest to members of NATO. Applications are handled by the Committee on International Exchange of the Conference Board of Associated Research Councils, 2101 Constitution Avenue N.W. in Washington, D.C.

The opportunities of the South East Asia Treaty Organization (SEATO) in educational exchange are primarily for nationals from the developing countries in Asia. Individuals may study at:

1. The Graduate School of Engineering in Bangkok, Thailand, which enrolls about 100 students each year.
2. Labor schools in Pakistan, the Philippines, and Thailand.
3. The Military Technical Training School in Thailand.
4. The Regional Community Development Technical Assistance Center in northeast Thailand.
5. The Teacher Development Center in Thailand.

SEATO also offers undergraduate and post-graduate scholarships, research fellowships, and exchange professorships in other countries.

United States candidates should apply to the Committee on International Exchange of the Conference Board of Associated Research Councils.

The Columbo Plan (members are the United States, Canada, Great Britain and the former members of the British Commonwealth in Asia) was set up in 1951 and functions primarily through bi-lateral agreements, particularly between Asian countries, for educational exchange and technical assistance.

The Organization of American States (OAS) is the major inter-governmental organization for inter-American affairs. Its founding charter of Bogota set up an Inter-American Cultural Council with a basic objective to promote educational, scientific, and cultural exchange, friendly relations and mutual understanding among American peoples. Its cultural programs, heirs of a considerable history of inter-American exchange planning, are handled by the Pan-American Union in Washington. Among its many programs and centers[4] are the following of particular interest:

1. Fellowships for nationals of member states, and for some nationals of non-member states upon conclusion of bilateral agreements, for study in Latin America.

2. The Lee S. Rowe Pan-American Fund for two years' study in the United States.

3. Fellowships for study at the Inter-American Rural Education Center in Rubio, Venezuela—this is a program for 50 students for ten months.

4. Study at the Fundamental Education Center (referred to as CREFAL) at Patzcuaro, Mexico—this program serves 20 students for a nine month period.

5. Study at the University of Puerto Rico for Caribbean area studies for 20 applicants for a two year period.

6. Study at the Inter-American Program for Urban and Regional Planning in Lima, Peru—for 40 students for a two year program.

There are also programs for study of economic integration in several countries: agrarian reform in Brazil; economic development in Fortaleza, Brazil; Indian community development in Bolivia and Guatemala; and journalism in Quito, Ecuador. Application to all of

---

[4] For further information, *see Study Abroad.*

these programs can be made to the Pan-American Union, Washington, D.C.

The many specialized inter-governmental organizations of European states which have developed since 1950 offer a limited number of fellowships and a large number of seminars for technical training and travel-study programs to students from member countries, and occasionally to nationals from non-member countries. For example, the Council of Europe, the most authoritative European organization, offers approximately 12 research fellowships of a year's duration to individuals from member countries, to individuals from non-member countries (who have signed the European Cultural Convention) and to refugees. Similar provisions apply to the programs of other European organizations.

The European Community offers a training fellowship, or *stagiere,* which lasts six months, to nationals of member countries. They are assigned to the bureaus of the director-generals of the Community secretariats in Brussels. Recommended students from Great Britain and the United States have occasionally been admitted to this program. In addition, students from the eighteen African associated member countries are eligible to enter training programs of 5 months at the European Community headquarters in Brussels, and can obtain fellowships of 9–12 months in any of the six member countries. Further information can be found in *Study Abroad* about these and other opportunities available from Euratom, the European Coal and Steel Community, the European Free Trade Association and other European organizations.

The Commonwealth Educational Conference held in 1959 at Oxford, England, established an interesting educational exchange program for the Commonwealth countries. One thousand fellowships will be available yearly, offered by each Commonwealth country to the nationals of the other Commonwealth countries for study in the former country's academic institutions.

Non-governmental International Organizations

There is a rather thick reference volume, *The Yearbook of International Organizations,*[5] which is devoted primarily to a listing of the many non-governmental international organizations. It contains in-

[5] Eyvind S. Tew, ed., *Yearbook of International Organizations 1964–5,* Union of International Associations (Brussels: Palais D'Egmont, 1964).

formation, by category, about the organizations' histories, structures, aims, recent activities, and publications. Many of these organizations offer opportunities to teachers and administrators for travel abroad in order to attend conferences and seminars, or to study or work abroad in educational or technical assistance programs. More comprehensive information about some of the educational exchange programs of private international organizations can be found in *Study Abroad*. Many of the international non-governmental organizations are coordinated through thirteen international unions and *their* coordinating body, the International Council of Scientific Unions.

Among these many organizations, a number are directed primarily toward education, such as the European Association of Teachers; the International Association for the Exchange of Students for Technical Experience (IAESTE); and the International Association of Students of Economics and Commercial Sciences.

One of these organizations, the International Association of Universities, was set up specifically to facilitate the enrollment of students at many diverse universities over the world. Founded in 1950, with headquarters in Paris, it provides a documentation and information service; it acts as a clearinghouse in collaboration with UNESCO; and it undertakes research on the equivalence of degrees.

Another organization, the International Bureau of Education, was established before World War II and is now also associated with UNESCO. It publishes some of the best work on comparative education.

A third international organization, the International Secretariat for Volunteer Services, was set up to coordinate and advise national groups supervising volunteers working in foreign or domestic service.

Programs of Some Member Governments in the United Nations

Leaning on, yet disavowing, the experience gained in administering empires in another era, France, Great Britain, and Germany have all developed extensive cultural programs, which are now concentrating more and more on the exchange of persons.[6]

---

[6] Philip H. Coombs, *The Fourth Dimension of Foreign Policy: Educational and Cultural Affairs* (New York: Harper & Row, Publishers, 1964). Chapter IV contains interesting material on which this section is partially based.

Pre-eminent among them is France which devotes one-half of the budget of the Foreign Ministry to cultural affairs and employs over 30,000 French teachers to serve abroad—a figure which is matched by an equivalent number teaching abroad under private auspices. The dividends of these monumental efforts are apparent. Nearly universal esteem for French culture exists among Africans and Asians, evident in their often faultless and elegant command of the French language, and the continuing French influence in the curriculum of their schools.

In addition, there are 10,000 French technical assistant experts abroad, 30,000 foreign students studying in France (two-thirds from developing countries, of which half are African), and the 800 cultural centers of the *Alliance Francaise* outside of France. (The United States group bearing the same name is independent of it.)

The French government waives tuition and provides meals, social security services, and other benefits for foreign students—including American students. It offers fourteen fellowships for study in French universities and forty assistantships for part-time teaching of English conversation classes in its secondary schools and teacher-training institutions. Its program, however, is directed primarily toward the developing countries, particularly toward its former African colonies, an orientation which has been criticized.[7]

The cultural program of the United Kingdom is administered by the hybrid British Council—a private, nearly autonomous arm of the government, funded by Parliament, in harmony with the Foreign Office, and separate from the British Information Service. The numbers of foreign students enrolled in British schools are comparable to those in the United States, but the proportion of the total enrollment is considerably greater in the United Kingdom. Foreign students are subsidized indirectly through their attendance at free tuition institutions. Rhodes and Marshall scholarships are offered to selected American students. In addition, the British government offers, under the administration of the Institute of International Education, a small number of grants, covering full or partial expenses, for Americans who wish to attend summer school programs of the

---

[7] The Institute of International Education has further information for United States citizens on these grants and those of other foreign governments.

universities of Birmingham (at Stratford-on-Avon), Edinburgh, London, and Oxford.[8]

The cultural program of the Federal Republic of Germany has undergone a number of shifts in gear. In 1950 the West German government set up the *Deutscher Akademischer Aufstauschdienst* (DAAD), an inter-university, autonomous exchange organization. Since 1960 it has made plans to strengthen its cultural programs, particularly for the developing countries. Goethe Institute, a private institution funded by the government, supplies German teachers and professors for service abroad and trains foreign teachers of German.

Germany continues to attract large numbers of foreign students. In 1962 its 24,000 foreign students made up 10 per cent of the total enrollment. The German government sponsors a number of programs which are open to Americans for study in Germany and to Germans for travel in the United States. Through these programs (1) a small group of German educators visits the United States to observe teacher training biennially; (2) students from the United States receive maintenance, tuition, and round trip travel for study in West Germany; (3) several universities—the University of Cologne, the Free University of Berlin, the Bavarian State University among others—support studies of American students during the academic and summer terms. All are administered by the Institute for International Education.

Mention should be made that the German government has a version of the Peace Corps, one of the first programs for overseas volunteer service formed after the United States Peace Corps.

Longer than many of the major powers, the Soviet Union has recognized the potential of an intelligent cultural relations program. As the Chinese and the British have done, they also have made maximum use of limited funds through careful planning. At present, there are about 25,000 foreign students enrolled in institutions of higher education in the Soviet Union and a number of students from the Soviet Union studying abroad (including, bizarrely enough, a number at the Vatican). Since the first agreement between the Soviet Union and the United States in 1958, its program has expanded

---

[8] Stewart Fraser, ed., *Government Policy and International Education* (New York: John Wiley & Sons, Inc., 1965). This is another rich source of information about the programs of other governments.

considerably. But numbers are carefully limited by the hair-splitting reciprocity inherent in a Cold War program.

Visits by American exchange students provide interesting and valuable glimpses of Soviet society. An American professor of Russian history, who has spent five months at the University of Moscow as a graduate student, is among recent rapporteurs.[9] Perhaps the most comprehensive analysis of the history and extent of the Soviet cultural programs is found in Professor Frederick Barghoorn's books *Soviet Foreign Propaganda* and *The Soviet Cultural Offensive*.[10]

Mainland China has directed an equally, if not more, astute program of cultural relations since World War II. Directing its invitations to the most vulnerable and potentially amenable audiences —Australians, Indian intellectuals, British and French scholars and journalists—it has allowed them a whirlwind visit which, despite its limitations, gives a valuable, because rare, picture of its society. Its program for the exchange of students is limited, especially for Chinese students. Students from underdeveloped countries come to China primarily for basic studies. The disillusionment caused by restrictions for African students is notorious. Students from advanced countries are usually accepted only for more specialized work. In general, the expansion and contraction of policy governing the cultural exchange program closely echoes the loosening and tightening of all Chinese policies.[11]

---

[9] Thomas T. Hammond and Dean Conger, "An American in Moscow," *National Geographic*, CXXIX (March, 1966), pp. 297–351.

[10] Frederick Barghoorn, *Soviet Foreign Propaganda* (Princeton, N.J.: Princeton University Press, 1964); and *The Soviet Cultural Offensive* (Princeton, N.J.: Princeton University Press, 1960).

[11] Herbert Passin, *Chinese Cultural Diplomacy* (New York: Frederick A. Praeger, 1962). Stewart Fraser, ed., Government Policy and International Education (New York: John Wiley & Son, Inc., 1965). Chapters 8 and 9 contain further information.

CHAPTER III

Programs of the United States Government

Although the title of this volume indicates the subject is *international* educational exchange, it is logical to assume that the readers of the Library of Education—either American or foreign—will be most interested in information on programs related to the United States. Thus from this point, the focus of the book will narrow somewhat.

History of Government Involvement

As the numbers of students, teachers and scholars travelling to and from the United States have increased, the involvement of the United States government has, unsurprisingly, grown accordingly. During the pre-war years, the government refrained from intruding on arrangements for educational exchange, partly in disinterest and partly in deference to the American consensus against government interference in the private domain. Later, it distinguished carefully the areas in which its involvement was legitimate—areas not covered by private agencies. Very recently, it has greatly expanded its role in education as a whole—and in international education in particular.

The official participation of the United States government in programs of cultural cooperation was initiated by its signing of the Convention for the Promotion of Inter-American Cultural Relations in 1936. But this was really only a formal ribbon-cutting, because the first substantial involvement, in inter-American cultural relations with Latin America, occurred several years later. The immediate cause for making Latin America the first geographical area to receive attention in this sphere was the overt Nazi propaganda program in Latin America in the 1930's. In the pre-war period, there were more German than American publications in Latin American libraries, and three-fourths of the 900 foreign schools were German. There were German professors in Latin America and

31

Latin American students in Germany. Runners-up in these categories were Italy and Japan, not the United States.[1]

Underlying the uneasiness of the United States with these statistics and the growing threat of Nazi Germany was a history of United States indifference toward Latin America, and the Latin American distrust of the imperialistic North Americans. Except for the efforts of the International Health Board of the Rockefeller Foundation and the inter-American exchanges supported by the Carnegie Foundation, the United States public and private institutions and universities had completely neglected Latin America. In 1938, the only volume on United States history that the Director of the Bogota, Colombia, National Library could find was on 17th century United States history.

In February, 1938, Franklin Delano Roosevelt suggested to his cabinet the necessity for a program of cultural relations with Latin America. In 1939, the Inter-departmental Committee of Cooperation was established, coordinating the efforts of twenty-five federal agencies. It administered educational exchange programs based on bi-lateral agreements. In 1947, the programs of this committee were transferred to the Department of State—which, in the meantime, had also created a Division of Cultural Affairs which handled cultural programs with Latin America. But the flow of its educational study-abroad programs was primarily one-way, from Latin America to the United States.

In October, 1938, a General Advisory Committee was appointed as consultant to the Division of Cultural Affairs. With the appointment of Vice President Henry Wallace to the Committee, the exchange programs lost an aristocratic bearing and gained an emphasis on technical assistance and economic and social goals. This enlargement of the program's focus was followed several years later by a geographical expansion when cultural programs with countries in the Near and Far East were added. For example, in 1942 the government made it possible for 1,700 Chinese students, stranded in the United States, to complete their studies and arranged for the exchange of teachers and technical missions to China.

---

[1] The material in this and following paragraphs on the history of the United States government's involvement is based on chapters in Charles A. Thomson and Walter H. C. Laves, *Cultural Relations and United States Foreign Policy, loc. cit.* (A valuable detailed history of this period.)

The General Advisory Committee was created to allow private citizens an opportunity to advise the government about its cultural activities. This opportunity for the private sector to advise the public sector was enlarged in 1939 when four conferences on cultural affairs, called by the Secretary of State, were held in Washington. The largest conference, attended by 600 university and college professors and leaders from 46 states, was on education.

In 1940, a third government office with Nelson Rockefeller, Coordinator of Inter-American Affairs as its chief, was created, perhaps with the intent to bypass the bureaucratic procedures of the Department of State and other agencies. It had a larger "exchange of persons" program than the Department of State, focusing particularly on journalists and broadcasting personnel. Some of its cultural activities were transferred to the Division of Cultural Affairs in 1943.

With the onset of World War II, the attention of the government turned to winning the war. The Office of War Information sponsored the travel of foreign journalists, radio commentators, and other public opinion makers to the United States and of American specialists to Great Britain, Australia, New Zealand, and South Africa. But its natural, primary purpose was information and propaganda rather than educational exchange. This predecessor of the United States Information Agency became part of the Division of Cultural Relations after the war.

Plans for cultural and educational cooperation were part of all peace plans at the end of the war, not just for humanitarian reasons but as an essential part of the future prevention of war. The two major steps taken to implement the plans were the establishment of the United Nations in 1945 and the passage of the Fulbright Amendment in 1946.

The Fulbright Program has been the core of the United States exchange program. The story of its beginning in 1946, when Senator Fulbright, himself once a Rhodes scholar, quietly proposed his amendment to the Property Act of 1944, has been told frequently.[2] He asked that Congress approve the use of foreign currency, resulting from the sale of U.S. surplus war property overseas, to finance

---

[2] Walter Johnson and Francis J. Colligan, *The Fulbright Program, A History* (Chicago: University of Chicago Press, 1965). This is the definitive discussion of the program.

the studies of American students abroad and the travel costs of foreign students to the United States. The innocuous-sounding amendment which would make Fulbright's surname a common noun, was passed without a flurry. The overseas studies of approximately 25,000 American and 37,500 foreign students have been supported by the Fulbright Amendment since 1948. In 1962, with the passage of the Fulbright-Hays Act, the 1946 amendment was repealed, but all its provisions were extended and enlarged.

From the early 1940's there was a steady undercurrent of controversy over the relationship of educational exchange to foreign policy. The controversy erupted in the Congressional hearings over the next major piece of legislation in this field—the Smith-Mundt Act of 1948. When educational exchange programs were set up with Latin American countries, some hoped they would exist for the sake of their cultural benefits alone, while others wanted exchange programs to assist the objectives of United States foreign policy in Latin America. This question of policy was resolved at that time by a compromise statement: cultural relations could deliberately assist the foreign policy goals of international understanding, the free exchange of information and peace, but could not be used to force the acceptance of more specific or non-cultural objectives.[3]

Such an issue is not unique to the United States. The governments of other nations have both cultural relations and information programs. Traditionally, educational and cultural programs overseas have been viewed as foreign policy weapons of another color. The degree and the way in which they are geared to foreign policy objectives has varied from country to country. Some of the reaction of the former colonies to the West can be understood in terms of the objectives and methods of the "mother" country with regard to the education of the citizens of the colony. Great Britain, France, Germany, and the Soviet Union have all in recent years administered their cultural relations and their information programs in separate bureaus.

In the United States the issue of the relation of educational and cultural programs to foreign policy objectives reappeared with the hearings for the United States Information and Educational Act of 1948, or the Smith-Mundt Act.

After a period of post-war complacency, Congress was aroused

---

[3] Thomson and Laves, *op. cit.,* pp. 43–44.

about the growing number of misrepresentations abroad concerning United States actions and American society. After long debate, a bill was passed which deepened the involvement of the government in the fields of information and educational exchange in an attempt to combat these false interpretations.

The advocates wanting a policy of educational and cultural relations relatively independent of foreign policy won. In order to keep educational exchange programs free of the specific foreign policy objectives of the information program, the two were carefully distinguished. The legislation also repeated the traditional maxim that private organizations should be utilized to the maximum degree. In fact, the government was forbidden to function in areas in which private groups could be equally competent. Yet another hazy area was clarified by the provision that technical assistance programs should be included with the educational interchange of persons, knowledges, and skills. Finally, the Act outlined programs, under the Secretary of State, for the exchange of persons, books, and other educational material, grants to American-sponsored schools, libraries, and community centers abroad, and grants to individuals, public or private non-profit organizations in the United States or abroad, for work which would further the basic aims of the cultural and educational program.[4]

Shortly thereafter, the Cold War intensified. The legal distinction made by the Smith-Mundt Act was nearly forgotten as educational exchange was subordinated to information, and educational exchange grants were awarded for their immediate political effect. They were even classified as "media services," for a period, in order to shortcut the existing bureaucratic procedures. When the United States Information Agency was established in 1953, only the efforts of Senators Fulbright, Mundt, and Hickenlooper saved educational exchange programs from being moved bodily into the information agency. The establishment of the United States Information Agency also brought the beginning of a peculiar division of responsibility which persists today. Although in the United States educational exchange programs are administered by the Department of State, overseas they are handled by the Cultural Affairs Officer who is

---

4 Philip H. Coombs, *The Fourth Dimension of Foreign Policy, Educational and Cultural Affairs, Council on Foreign Relations* (New York: Harper & Row, Publishers, 1964), pp. 30–32.

under the direct authority of the United States Information Agency and thus reports to two masters in Washington. The absurdity of this arrangement has frequently been noted. The first full-length study was written by Charles Frankel and was published in 1965. In *The Neglected Aspect of Foreign Affairs,* he discusses in detail the organization and some of the difficulties presented by this arrangement.[5]

Despite the publicity given to the "people-to-people" approach and the creation of the Eisenhower fellowships, during the Eisenhower administration educational exchange programs hit a low point. Appropriations declined from $16 million in 1951 to $10 million in 1955. The number of American and foreign individuals receiving government grants declined from 7,200 in 1951 to 4,900 in 1954.[6] One of the more productive measures of these years, insofar as educational exchange programs are concerned, was the passage of the Agricultural Trade Development and Assistance Act in 1954, frequently referred to as P.L. 480. This legislation was directed primarily toward financing foreign purchases of agricultural surpluses. But it allowed foreign currency that was in the United States possession overseas and which had accumulated as a result of these foreign purchases to be used to support educational exchange arrangements as well as American studies abroad. Although this provided real benefits, it did have two undesirable side effects (as did the Fulbright Amendment): (1) rationalizing a lower budgeting of dollars for exchange programs in Congress, and (2) producing geographical distortions in these programs, mirroring the emphasis of the United States aid programs.[7]

Among the understandings reached in 1955 at the Summit Conference was the agreement to increase educational and cultural relations between the United States and the Soviet Union. This was implemented in January of 1958 with the signing of the helpful and historic First Soviet-American Exchange Agreement, which was to be renewed biennially, and which permitted a modest variety of reciprocal exchanges. They were negotiated by the Department of State but were financed and administered by private organizations.[8]

---

[5] Charles Frankel, *The Neglected Aspect of Foreign Affairs* (Washington, D.C.: Brookings Institution, 1965).

[6] Coombs, *op. cit.,* pp. 35–36.

[7] *Ibid.,* pp. 38–39.

[8] *Ibid.,* pp. 39–41.

Secretary of State Christian Herter authorized the establishment of the present bureau handling and coordinating educational exchange programs in the Department of State, that is, the Bureau of Educational and Cultural Affairs. The bureau was organized on geographical lines. Its significance was recognized in 1961 when President John F. Kennedy created the office of Assistant Secretary of State for Educational and Cultural Affairs.[9]

Another important piece of legislation, the Fulbright-Hays or Mutual Educational and Cultural Exchange Act of 1961, replaced previous legislation. This Act broadened the functions of the screening and executive body, the Board of Foreign Scholarships, and created a United States Advisory Commission on Educational and Cultural Affairs. It called for the establishment of centers for intercultural communication, such as the East-West Center in Hawaii, increased the numbers of cultural presentations by foreign performers in the United States to balance the flow of American performers travelling abroad, and suggested greater collaboration with the related work of international organizations.

At the beginning of President Kennedy's administration, task forces were assigned to study the depth and breadth of the international programs of American universities and of the educational exchange programs of the United States. Historic studies resulted[10] which influenced the direction of American efforts in the years to come. At the beginning of President Lyndon B. Johnson's second term, another assessment was made. In his Smithsonian speech on September 16, 1965, President Johnson promised an enlargement of efforts in this area of international education. In his statement to Congress in February, 1966, he suggested the outlines which such an enlarged effort might take. He called for the creation of a Center for Educational Cooperation in the Department of Health, Education, and Welfare, repeating the call made by John Gardner in *AID and the Universities,* for the creation of a new agency geared to handle technical and educational cooperation.[11]

Qualified students can expect further help from the government

9 Philip Coombs was the first man to hold this position. His book, *The Fourth Dimension of Foreign Policy Educational and Cultural Affairs,* is based on his experience. The present incumbent is Charles Frankel.

10 Among them *The University and World Affairs,* Report of the Committee on the University and World Affairs, J. L. Morill, Chairman (New York: Ford Foundation, 1961).

11 Gardner, John, *AID and the Universities* (New York: Education and World Affairs, 1964).

program. There should be many more dollars available for general educational exchange and there will be increased opportunities for exchange of teachers. President Johnson has suggested a goal of 1,000 "school-to-school partnerships"; an American Education Placement Service to place "school and college teachers eager to serve abroad"; an expanded United States Summer Teaching Corps; and intensified efforts to assist the teaching of English abroad. Many of the ideas embodied in President Johnson's proposal for an International Educational and Health Act of 1966 were suggested by specialists in the United States who were consulted individually in the fall of 1965 and collectively at the White House Conference on International Cooperation in December, 1965.

From 1949 to 1966 the degree of government involvement and numbers of government grantees, with the exception noted in the mid-1950's, has steadily, even spectacularly, increased and seems unlikely to slow down.

Without going deeply into the details of the changing and compartmentalized structures of the government agencies handling educational exchange programs, it may be helpful to indicate what the jurisdiction and relationships are between the foremost government agencies. Also in order to assist further inquiry, the major categories of opportunities at all levels—from the undergraduate to the specialist—will be mentioned.

Department of State

The purposes of the educational and cultural exchange programs of the Department of State are (1) to deepen the understanding between the people of the United States and people of other countries, (2) to promote international cooperation in order to support educational and cultural development, and (3) to encourage peaceful relations between the United States and other countries. From 1949 to 1966 the Department of State has lent support to over 100,000 American and foreign students and teachers abroad.

The administration of all the educational exchange programs of the Department of State—and the coordination and varying degrees of administration of the programs of other government agencies—are handled by the Bureau of Educational and Cultural Affairs. An Assistant Secretary of State directs its geographical offices and the

Office of Multilateral and Special Activities, Office of United States Programs and Services, Office of Cultural Presentations, the staff for Public Information and Reports, and the staff for Policy Review and Coordination. The Secretariat of the United States National Commission for UNESCO is also housed in this bureau. The Bureau of Educational and Cultural Affairs publishes a *conversational* detailed annual report of its programs, entitled *Educational and Cultural Diplomacy,*[12] and a very helpful pamphlet, *Educational and Cultural Exchange Opportunities,* for citizens wishing to apply to one of its programs.[13]

There are several advisory commissions and coordinating committees connected with this bureau. The Board of Foreign Scholarships, a distinguished panel of private consultants established in 1946, supervises all programs under the Fulbright-Hays Act and makes the final selection of recipients of Fulbright grants. It relies on screening by the Committee on International Exchange of the Conference Board of Associated Research Councils for American doctoral and post-doctoral applicants, and on screening by the Institute of International Education for undergraduate and graduate students from the United States. It publishes annual reports and the very readable *Teacher and Scholar Abroad—First Person Reports* which contains frank statements of the experiences of American grantees overseas and of foreign grantees in the United States.[14]

The United States Advisory Commission on International Education and Cultural Affairs (some members are distinguished private citizens) makes recommendations to the Department of State, some in the form of reports. After its creation in 1961, the Advisory Commission asked John Gardner to direct a study of United States educational exchange programs. The resulting publication, *Beacon of Hope,* concluded that, although a few foreign grantees left the United States with negative attitudes, the program, as a whole, was overwhelmingly successful. It included suggestions that have had great influence on the analyses and proposals which have followed

---

[12] United States Department of State, *Educational and Cultural Diplomacy 1964* (Washington, D.C.: U.S. Government Printing Office, 1965).

[13] United States Department of State, Bureau of Educational and Cultural Affairs, *Educational and Cultural Exchange Opportunities,* Publication #7543, International Information and Cultural Series 83, revised edition (Washington, D.C.: Department of State, April 1965).

[14] *Teacher and Scholar Abroad—First Person Reports* (Washington, D.C.: United States Government Printing Office, 1964).

it.[15] In 1965 the Advisory Commission began publication of a valuable quarterly *International Educational and Cultural Exchange.*

The selection of applicants and administration of programs abroad is handled by the Cultural Affairs Officer or the Educational Affairs Officer or the Public Affairs Officer in the American Embassy in each country, and by bi-national commissions. Sometimes known as Fulbright Foundations, these commissions are set up by bi-lateral agreements to review applications and to administer American-related educational and cultural programs in the country. Some bi-lateral agreements now provide for a sharing of the costs of educational exchange programs, previously paid entirely by the United States government. This may bring a greater reflection of the interests of the foreign countries into educational exchange programs.

The Department of State offers different kinds of opportunities for an educational experience abroad. It helps citizens of the United States to study, to teach, to do advanced research, to lecture, or to consult abroad; it helps individuals from many other lands to have similar experiences in the United States. Each of its programs is administered with the assistance of private agencies, advisory committees made up of private citizens, and universities. The vital skeletons of these programs are outlined below.

Grants for United States citizens wanting to study abroad. Students from the United States may apply for grants to do graduate study abroad with an educational institution overseas. In addition to grants provided by the Fulbright-Hays Act, grants are available through the Inter-American Cultural Convention for study in Latin American countries. Fulbright-Hays grants, available for a period of one year, are usually not extended. They may cover transportation, tuition, maintenance, and incidental expenses. Although they do not cover the expenses of dependents, other benefits, such as those from the GI Bill, may be received concurrently. Usually, students are paid in the currency of the country in which their study will be undertaken. Expenses in Latin America are met in a different way under the Inter-American Cultural Convention. The United States government pays travel expenses; the host country pays tuition, mainte-

---

15 United States Advisory Commission on International Educational and Cultural Affairs, *A Beacon of Hope—The Exchange-of-Persons Program* (Washington, D.C.: U.S. Government Printing Office, 1963).

nance, and incidental expenses. In sum this amount is not always sufficient.[16]

Applicants must have the equivalent of a bachelor's degree. Their project must be sound and one which the country's resources and academic regulations will allow. They must have enough ability in the country's language to be able to carry out study. (Allowances are sometimes made for languages rarely taught in the United States.) Applicants must be healthy and, usually, under 35 years of age. Undergraduate applicants may apply to their campus Fulbright advisers or to the Institute of International Education, 809 United Nations Plaza, New York, New York, between May and October 31 for awards which will be used the following year. It is important to emphasize that there is an early deadline, as many students fail to realize that they must apply far ahead and thus can miss out on the opportunity. Applications are reviewed by campus committees who nominate special State scholars (two from each state). Then the Institute of International Education's National Screening Committee reviews all applications. Final decisions on Fulbright-Hays and Inter-American Cultural Convention awards are made by the Board of Foreign Scholarships.

Grants for study in the United States.   Most, but not all, of the grants administered by the Department of State available to foreign students who want to study in the United States are on the graduate level. They are awarded for one year but sometimes they are extended if certain conditions in the student's academic program, academic sponsorship, or financial support are met. Some grants cover all expenses likely to be encountered—travel, maintenance, room and board, books and supplies, tuition and fees. Other grants cover only travel expenses. There are grants available also in Burma, Greece, Italy, Turkey, and certain Latin American countries for attendance at American-sponsored schools abroad.

The foreign student must have an academic background and sufficient command of the English language to allow him to undertake studies at the university level in the United States. He must be healthy and, usually, between the ages of 18 and 35. He may apply to the United States Educational Commission or Foundation in his

---

[16] The information in this and other paragraphs on Department of State programs is based on the extremely helpful "Educational and Cultural Exchange Opportunities" mentioned above.

capital city but, if none exists, to the American Embassy or Consulate of his country. The Board of Foreign Scholarships makes the final evaluation. Any institution in the United States wishing to aid or enroll foreign students should contact the Institute of International Education, 809 United Nations Plaza, New York, New York.

Teaching abroad: United States citizens.   There are three kinds of grants for those in the United States wishing to teach abroad— university teaching grants and two types of secondary and elementary teaching grants.

Citizens of the United States can teach or lecture abroad in institutions of higher learning under the Fulbright-Hays Act. Although sometimes granted for a summer session or a single semester, grants are mostly made for a one year period. Grants, paid in foreign currency and which include transportation and living expenses, are determined by the cost of living and the number of grantees going to a particular country. Grants paid in United States currency are usually considered as supplementary to other funds received from the university in the host country.

Applicants should have the equivalent of the Ph.D. degree in training or status; one year of college teaching experience; and the ability to lecture in the native language of Austria, Belgium, France, Germany, Italy, or Latin America (unless the subject is American literature or English). In other countries, he can lecture in English. Applications for Fulbright-Hays lecture grants should be made to the Conference Board of Associated Research Councils, 2101 Constitution Avenue, N.W., Washington 25, D.C. by March 1 to April 15 if to be used in New Zealand or Latin America in the spring or summer term of the next year; or between June 1 and August 1 if to be used elsewhere in the fall term of the next calendar year. Applications are first reviewed by screening committees composed of experts in the various disciplines, then by the Committee on International Exchange of Persons of the Conference Board of Associated Research Councils, and finally by the Board of Foreign Scholarships. Applications are kept in a register by the Conference Board Committee. If unfilled positions remain or special requests are made by the American embassies, selection is made either from this register or by open recruitment.

The Fulbright-Hays legislation also provides for grants to United States citizens to teach in a foreign national school or in an American-sponsored school abroad—on a level equivalent to the elementary or secondary system of the United States. These programs are of two types: direct interchange of positions and the more common exchange program system.

The "one-for-one" interchanges of positions are found only between the United States and certain countries in Western Europe, Latin America, and the Pacific area. Applicants must have a bachelor's degree, three years' teaching experience and be presently teaching in an elementary, secondary, teacher-training, or junior college which is ready to receive a foreign teacher in exchange. Fluency is desirable, and sometimes required, in the language of the host country. Possession of a master's degree is sometimes required also. These grants usually provide for travel and, except for arrangements with the United Kingdom (in which salaries are paid by the home institution), necessary living expenses are provided.

The more common non-reciprocal exchange of teachers program requires that applicants have a bachelor's degree, and three years' teaching experience. Here again a master's degree is sometimes required. Fluency in the language of the host country is desirable and sometimes necessary. Grants cover travel and living expenses abroad.

In addition to these academic year programs, there are summer programs available to United States teachers of foreign languages, the classics, and some of the social sciences. These programs allow for round trip international travel for professional study and intensive training in France, Germany, Italy, India, and a few Latin American countries.

All teachers who wish to apply for the above mentioned programs should contact the United States Office of Education, Department of Health, Education, and Welfare, Washington 25, D.C. before October 15 of the calendar year prior to the academic year in which they wish to teach.

Teaching in the United States: foreign nationals.   Foreign nationals who wish to lecture in a university or college in the United States, for the most part, receive only grants for their international travel under the Fulbright-Hays Act. Other expenses are usually met by the host school and occasionally by United States government funds available under other legislation.

These appointments are usually for one academic year. Applicants must be citizens of whatever countries the United States universities and colleges stipulate and the applicant's background must be acceptable to the potential host institutions. They must have a good command of English. Again applications may be obtained through the United States Educational Foundation, Embassy, or Consulate located in the foreign country. The Board of Foreign Scholarships makes the final selection.

Colleges and universities in the United States may communicate directly with any individuals abroad whom they wish to employ, and suggest that they get in touch with the American Embassy about obtaining a travel grant and funds for other expenses. Those colleges and universities without specific candidates may contact the Conference Board of Associated Research Councils, 2101 Constitution Avenue, N.W., Washington, D.C., if they want help in finding a visiting lecturer or professor.

The Fulbright-Hays Act also provides funds to support foreign nationals who wish to teach and observe in the United States at the elementary and secondary school levels. There are grants which are used for direct interchange of a foreign and American teacher for one academic year, and for study and observation of the organization and administration of the elementary and secondary schools in the United States. Although usually for six months, the grants are sometimes of longer or shorter duration. Grants for direct interchange of teachers cover only international travel with other expenses covered by the salary from the school in the United States. Grants for study and observation sometimes include both travel and living expenses. Applicants for these grants must have taught for three straight years on a full-time basis, unless they are administrators or supervisors. They must have an adequate knowledge of English and be between 25 and 40 years of age. Their intention must be to remain in the field of education. Foreign nationals should apply to the American Embassy or Consulate in their own countries. American schools wishing to receive teachers from other lands should write to the Teacher Exchange Section, Division of International Education, United States Office of Education, Department of Health, Education, and Welfare, Washington 25, D.C. After candidates have been nominated by their American Embassy or Consulate, in conjunction with the local Ministry of Education or the United States Educational Commission or Foundation; the Board of

Foreign Scholarships of the Department of State makes the final selection.

Research abroad for citizens of the United States.   Scholars, specialists, and lecturers in the United States who wish to work abroad may apply for Fulbright-Hays grants. Grants for advanced research usually provide for the travel and living expenses of the grantee, paid in foreign currency, but no provision is made for dependents. Candidates must have the equivalent of a Ph.D. degree when they apply as well as a knowledge of the language of the country, and a planned research project that is acceptable. Their application should be sent to the Conference Board of Associated Research Councils, 2101 Constitution Avenue, N.W., Washington, D.C. between March 1 and April 15 for research projects in Australia, New Zealand and Latin America beginning in the spring or summer of the next academic year and between June 1 and August 1 for research projects beginning in the fall academic term of the next calendar year in all other countries. Applications are reviewed by screening committees and selected by the Board of Foreign Scholarships. For lecture and consultation abroad, grants are made to outstanding American specialists. Qualifications, compensations, and applications vary. Recommendations are made by universities, foundations, professional associations, and former grantees, with the concurrence of the Department of State and the Foreign Service officials in the recipient country. Grants, both full and partial, are administered by the Division of Americans Abroad, Bureau of Educational and Cultural Affairs, Department of State, Washington 25, D.C. They are usually for three or more months and frequently for work in more than one country.

Visiting scholars and specialists.   There are a number of plans for scholars, specialists, and leaders in the United States and abroad to travel in and out of the United States under the Fulbright-Hays legislation. These grants are usually of short duration in order to broaden the opportunity for international experience to a greater number of individuals.

Foreign post-doctoral scholars may receive support for undertaking advanced research in United States universities for periods varying from three to twelve months. International travel expenses are usually met by the government, other expenses by the host institution. But in exceptional circumstances the United States government will often pay these expenses.

Candidates must be citizens of countries having exchange programs with the United States, must be acceptable to the host institution, and have a command of the English language. Necessary information may be obtained from the United States Educational Commission or Foundation, or the American Embassy or Consulate. The Board of Foreign Scholarships makes the final selection. If a college or university in the United States wishes to have a foreign national undertake research at its institution, it should make contact with that individual and have him get in touch with the American Embassy, or else write a general inquiry to the Conference Board of Associated Research Councils, 2101 Constitution Avenue, N.W., Washington, D.C.

Foreign nationals may also receive support for specialized training or practical professional experience in the United States under the provisions of the Fulbright-Hays Act. These grants, which usually cover all expenses for about 600 individuals each year over a period of four to six months, take a number of forms. Visiting specialists travel in groups, which are frequently multi-national, or they may work as individuals alongside their American counterparts in offices, libraries, radio and television stations; they may attend special seminars in colleges and universities. The programming of these visits is handled by the Department of State, by universities, and by professional organizations such as the Experiment in International Living, the Institute for International Education, the African-American Institute, and the Governmental Affairs Institute.

Candidates are required to have an adequate educational and professional background in terms of the proposed project, citizenship in a country having an applicable exchange program, and a good command of English. There is no open competition, but, rather, selection is by invitation from the Board of Foreign Scholarships of persons nominated by American Embassies and Consulates. Organizations in the United States wishing to participate in any phase of this program should get in touch with the Bureau of Educational and Cultural Affairs of the Department of State.

Other grants for foreign nationals.   Under the rubric of "Foreign Leader" grants, the Department of State yearly invites about 900 distinguished foreign nationals who are leaders in journalism, labor, governmental affairs, civic and community affairs, education, social welfare, and the fine arts to travel in ten or twelve cities in the United States. Here they meet their American counterparts; they observe American society for thirty to sixty days, usually as individuals but occasionally in groups. American Embassies and Consulates make these nominations with the Department of State finally selecting the potential guests. Again, American organizations wishing to support, confer with, or entertain these leaders should write to the Bureau of Educational and Cultural Affairs, Department of State, Washington, D.C.

The final category of grants available to foreign nationals is a growing one having significant potential. These are grants which are available to about 800 young leaders, professional leaders, but more especially to students, for visitation to the United States for a thirty to forty day period. Frequently these young people travel in groups (such as a group of Asian student leaders); they usually stay with American families, visit college campuses, and sometimes have discussions with officials in the Department of State. Escort interpreters accompany such groups. Full grants provide transportation and living expenses. Interested students can apply to the American Consulate or Embassy in their own country, which makes nominations that are sent to the Department of State. Organizations interested in cooperating with this program should write the Division for Visitors from Abroad, Bureau of Educational and Cultural Affairs, Department of State, Washington, D.C.

Additional programs of the Department of State. In addition to these programs for educational and professional exchange which the Department of State finances, it also:

1. Programs the visits of nearly 1,400 individuals who receive financial support from private organizations;
2. finances projects to strengthen foreign area and language training programs in the United States (these are administered by the Office of Education and supervised by the Board of Foreign Scholarships);
3. finances American-sponsored schools in 50 countries;
4. supports junior year abroad programs of United States colleges and universities;
5. contributes funds to seminars at these institutions for foreign students and visiting youth leaders;
6. finances groups having youth programs;

7. supports projects furthering the establishment of workshops and chairs for American studies abroad;[17]
8. undertakes other projects which promote its objectives;
9. (under a Cultural Presentations program, initiated in 1954 and intensified in late 1963) sponsors tours by creative and performing artists, athletes, and arranges for international representation in festivals, competitions, meetings, and exhibitions.

The Department of State has a unique exchange program with the Soviet Union and East Europe. The Soviet exchange program, initiated in 1958 and renewed in 1966, is a carefully planned and executed reciprocal program in an exchange of scholars and performers. In view of the restrictions on travel between the United States and these "iron curtain" countries, these exchange programs make a very significant contribution toward international communication. An unusual feature is that the Soviet and East Europe exchanges staff of the Department of State publishes reports semi-annually.[18]

The Department of State maintains Reception Centers at all major ports of entry to the United States to meet the incoming visitors at docks and airports; to arrange hotel accommodations for them; to make any professional appointments necessary; and to offer them local hospitality.

Agency for International Development (AID)

The chameleon-like governmental operation now known as the Agency for International Development[19] handles the foreign aid and technical assistance programs of the United States which, although existing before World War II, began with the Marshall Plan in Europe and the Point Four program in Greece and Turkey after the war.

Per se, the Agency for International Development (AID) has a strong involvement in education, particularly in the educational

---

[17] *See* Walter Johnson, *American Studies Abroad,* U.S. Advisory Commission on International Educational and Cultural Affairs (Washington, D.C.: U.S. Government Printing Office, 1965).

[18] United States Department of State, Soviet and Eastern Europe Exchanges Staff, *Exchanges With the Soviet Union and Eastern Europe* (Washington, D.C.: United States Printing Office).

[19] Previous manifestations were the Foreign Operations Administration and International Cooperation Administration.

development projects which have become the principal focus of so many persons and organizations involved in international education. It has a role in the "exchange-of-persons" movement because its technical assistance programs bring foreign nationals to the United States and send American technicians to other countries on a consultation or supervisory basis. These programs are handled primarily by agencies of the United States government but also by contract with American universities.

Each year the International Training Division of AID brings about 5,000 "participants" to the United States for training and sends about 2,000 "participants" to other countries for training and education, and it sends about 5,000 technical advisers overseas.[20] About 300 persons are sent abroad as educational advisers.[21] Large numbers of these turn out to be teachers. Edward W. Weidner lists the most frequent kinds of teaching as: (1) direct teaching while acting as a substitute teacher; (2) direct teaching in a demonstration class; and (3) teaching of intermediary groups such as teachers or the teachers of teachers. Further information on the conditions and results of these kinds of assignments abroad can be found in the Weidner study referred to in the bibliography. Training areas are in agriculture, labor, industry, mining, transportation, public health, housing, public administration, community development, public safety, and atomic energy—in short, in the technical skills prized by newly independent nations wishing to accelerate their economic development. The programs are frequently handled by private firms, universities, and other governmental agencies (such as the Department of Agriculture, Department of Commerce, Federal Aviation Agency, Federal Communications Commission, Housing and Home Finance Agency), with AID frequently providing the financial support for the training staffs.

AID also has contracts with over 100 universities in the United States involving their developmental overseas projects in more than thirty countries. In a significant analysis, John Gardner notes that not one American in a hundred, or even a thousand, realizes that this unique partnership between the government and the universities

---

[20] United States Department of State, Bureau of Educational and Cultural Affairs, *Some U.S. Government Agencies Involved in International Activities* (Washington, D.C.: U.S. Government Printing Office, 1963).

[21] Coombs, *op. cit.,* p. 61.

exists.[22] His report discusses the difficulties which these relationships entail, reflecting the perennial difficulties of the Agency of International Development. He suggests a number of remedies, among them the creation of a semi-autonomous governmental institute for educational and technical cooperation—which was echoed in the President's suggestions for an International Health and Education Act of 1966. Gardner suggested that participant training programs be better defined, with better selection criteria and entailing a longer period of training in the university. He also recommended that English speaking ability not be a criterion for admission, but rather that intensive training in English be offered on arrival.

Even though the educational and technical exchange programs of AID are necessarily diverse, a goodly portion of them revolve around teacher development. The programs involve students in the United States and teachers abroad in such a way as to strengthen the basic and fundamental sectors of developing countries.

United States Information Agency (USIA)

The United States Information Agency is involved indirectly in two kinds of cooperation with the international exchange of teachers and students. The first has evolved historically from the vague separation of powers when the government's program of cultural relations was in its developing stage. With the creation of the United States Information Agency in 1953, responsibility for the screening and selection of foreign candidates for Fulbright grants was given to the Cultural Affairs Officer, in the American Embassy in each country. The Cultural Affairs Officer reports to the United States Information Agency. This system persists today, and is the subject of Charles Frankel's study, *The Neglected Aspect of Foreign Affairs, American Educational and Cultural Policy Abroad,* written before he became Assistant Secretary of State for Educational and Cultural Affairs. In each country the Cultural Affairs Officer (or the Public Affairs or Educational Affairs Officer) frequently sits on the United States Educational Commission—if there is one.

---

22 John W. Gardner, *AID and the Universities.* A Report to the Administrator of the Agency for International Development. (New York: Education and World Affairs, 1964), p. 1. Mr. Gardner, president of the Carnegie Corporation when he wrote this, is now Secretary of the Department of Health, Education, and Welfare.

The other related function of USIA is its administration and staffing of bi-national centers in many countries. At these cross-cultural meeting places, teachers from the United States are frequently employed to teach English. Persons interested in further information should get in touch with the Employment Branch Personnel Division, United States Information Agency, Washington, D.C.

Peace Corps

Fifty per cent of all Peace Corps volunteers are teaching abroad. The others are involved in rural and urban community development, health projects, agriculture, and public works. In 1966 there are 10,000 volunteers in 46 countries, and plans have been made to increase this number markedly.

Probably no program captured the imagination of young Americans more effectively than did the Peace Corps. The small group of original volunteers met ridicule and scorn in the early days. However, over the years, the Peace Corps turned out to be highly effective, if only in presenting a truly altruistic image of the United States countering the imperialistic picture painted by many. Every other volunteer now teaches. Thus the Corps offers an obvious opportunity for young teachers to learn and serve abroad. Most of the teaching volunteers are in Africa. In Ethiopia, they compose one-half of the secondary education staff of the country.

Many of the volunteers have gone back to school; many others are teaching in the United States after finishing their term of service in the Peace Corps. At Cardoza High School in Washington, D.C., returned Peace Corps volunteers are staffing a special program for the culturally deprived. Some municipal school systems have employed returned volunteers prior to their becoming certified as teachers. Their teaching in the schools where they are employed is accepted as a substitute for practice-teaching. Some universities have begun to give the equivalent of practice teaching credits just for Peace Corps experience itself. Other school systems are eager to recruit returned volunteers to staff community colleges, which are increasing in number. (In New York in the summer of 1966, a special program will train returned volunteers intensively just for this purpose.) These instances are part of the growing groundswell of a desire to utilize the international experience of the returned volunteer in order to strengthen the educational system of the United States.

Abroad, the Peace Corps programs are turning increasingly to community organization projects, which are fundamentally necessary for the economic development of the country involved. This has been partly an outgrowth of the recent emphasis upon community organization and development within the United States.

Individuals interested in applying to the Peace Corps are required formally only to be over 18. Application forms may be obtained by writing The Peace Corps, Washington 25, D.C. The decision to accept a Peace Corps candidate for training is made after tests are taken. These tests are offered frequently throughout the year in many cities.

The East-West Center

Although many universities and colleges have developed area studies and international relations programs since World War II, none are quite like the Center for Cultural and Technical Interchange between East and West, or "East-West Center," which is located in the midst of the University of Hawaii in Honolulu. Authorized by the Mutual Security Act of 1960, it was intended to promote mutual understanding among countries in the Asian-Pacific area and the United States, and to foster better American relations with the East.

The East-West Center has many programs for studies and for conferences for students on many strata. At its Institute for Student Interchange, approximately 200 Asian and 100 American students each year begin a two-year program—usually on the graduate level —in courses at the University of Hawaii. Field study of six to nine months follows—on the United States mainland for Asians; in Asia, for students from the United States.

Through the Teacher Interchange Program, Asian and American teachers study for one year at joint seminars in Hawaii, finishing in the summer with appropriate exchange programs in the United States and Asia. In the Academic Year Institute, Asian science and mathematics teachers on the secondary level do non-degree work for a year, with summer work in the United States. Beginning with the summer of 1966 under the Summer Institute for Asian studies, American teachers and administrators can attend a summer institute at the University of Hawaii. In the Language Teacher Program, ten participants from the United States spend fifteen months in Hawaii and Asia learning Japanese or Chinese with the purpose of establishing courses in these languages at home upon their return. In addition to a "junior year abroad," there are many other programs offered: technical training, accelerated student opportunities, advanced scholar study, and conferences for senior scholars. Further information about these programs can be obtained directly from the East-West Center.

Programs of the United States Office of Education, Department of Health, Education, and Welfare (HEW)

The chief international function of the Office of Education, Department of Health, Education, and Welfare is ". . . to foster the development of educational institutions so that they meet the needs of American society in a rapidly changing world."[23]

With the appointment of John Gardner to the position of Secretary of the Department of Health, Education, and Welfare, and with the radical proposals made by President Johnson for comprehensive new legislation in 1966, in the fields of international education and health, the already heavily committed Department of Health, Education, and Welfare assumes a vastly more complex and decidedly more crucial role in the international affairs of government. It seems that, under the leadership of President Johnson, the United States is destined to enter more forcefully and substantially into the most far-reaching of all welfare states. HEW, already deeply involved in the whole spectrum of governmental programs in international education, was suggested by the President in 1966 as the logical coordinator of United States efforts in the fields of cultural, educational, intellectual, and to some extent, technical exchange (in the field of health).

The exchange of teachers program has been "outstandingly successful."[24] One of the reasons for sending people abroad is to have them make a contribution to their community upon their return. This rationale can nowhere be more fully realized than when teachers who have studied and taught in Paris, France, return to their class-

---

[23] *The U.S. Office of Education: A New International Dimension* (New York: Education and World Affairs, 1964), p. 1.

[24] Robert Blum, *Cultural Affairs and Foreign Relations* (Englewood Cliffs, N.J.: The American Assembly, 1963), p. 91.

rooms in Paris, Illinois. *Teacher and Scholar Abroad, First Person Reports of the U.S. Exchange Programs,* published by the Board of Foreign Scholarships, orchestrates this theme most effectively in remarks of varying intensity of teachers who have travelled and studied abroad.

The United States Office of Education administers the exchange programs of teachers supported by funds under the Fulbright-Hays Act.[25] But it also handles some of the exchange programs provided for by the National Defense Education Act and the programs of the Agency for International Development. Thus, under the direction of the Office of Education teachers are interchanged directly between the United States and certain countries in Europe, Latin America, and the Pacific area; United States teachers are sent abroad to study and teach; and foreign teachers are brought to observe schools in the United States. Moreover, foreign specialists are invited to advise their United States counterparts in curriculum development and training and graduate students and senior scholars from language and area study centers in the United States are sent abroad. Individuals wishing to learn more about these opportunities should write the Teacher Exchange Section, Office of Education, Department of Health, Education, and Welfare, or consult *Teacher Exchange Opportunities and Summer Seminars*[26] which describes these and other opportunities. It also contains helpful lists of grants by countries and subjects.

Other aspects of international education are grist for the mills of many other bureaus of the Office of Education. In the Offices of the Bureaus of Educational Assistance Programs (BEAP), Educational Research and Development (BERD), and International Education (BIE), civil servants are compiling information on foreign educational systems; doing cross-cultural research; maintaining a library of American textbooks for visiting foreign educators; preparing guides for the interpretation of foreign academic credentials; arranging programs for individuals from the developing countries at American institutions who have come to the United States under the auspices of AID; recruiting Americans for overseas service under UNESCO and AID; and no doubt performing other relevant chores.

The international teacher development programs have great im-

---

[25] *Ibid.,* pp. 60–65.

[26] United States Department of Health, Education, and Welfare, *Teacher Exchange Opportunities and Summer Seminars* (Washington, D.C.: U.S. Government Printing Office, 1963).

pact by bringing foreign teachers to the United States to study the educational system through a planned program of observation, seminars, and homestays. Dean Stiles of the School of Education, University of Wisconsin, said this of his 1962 program: "because the program included twenty-five educational leaders from sixteen different countries, the University of Wisconsin perhaps gained most . . . we want you to know that you leave with us a part of your sparkling dedication to truth, to freedom, and to humanity . . . wherever you may be because you have been with us, you now will be of Wisconsin also."[27]

In 1964, an analysis of the Office of Education was made by Education and World Affairs which contained a number of suggestions for the strengthening of its international capabilities.[28] Many of these recommendations have been implemented. As the traditionally unviolated sanctuary of state, local, and private education falls more and more into the federal domain, its international dimension can only swell in step with the inflation of the international dimension of all American institutions.

Programs of Other Government Agencies

In addition to the enormous trafficking in international educational exchange directed by the Department of State and the Department of Health, Education, and Welfare, many other offices of governmental agencies administer educational and technical exchange programs. Many of these programs are concerned with technical training of short duration, and thus are only on the boundaries of this volume's preserve. There are two valuable guides to the reader interested in probing further. Philip Coombs has devised neat diagrammatic summaries of the international educational activities of the federal government;[29] the Department of State has compiled information on all the international activities of the agencies of the federal government.[30]

---

27 "International Teacher Development Program" The Coordinator's Report (Madison, Wis.: The University of Wisconsin, 1962), p. 3.

28 *The United States Office of Education: A New International Dimension* (New York: Education and World Affairs, 1964).

29 Coombs, *op. cit.,* pp. 144–48. Table 1 indicates which of about 50 categories of educational exchange the major agencies undertake, while Table 2 cross-indexes these functions to other governmental offices.

30 United States Department of State, Bureau of Educational and Cultural Affairs, *Some United States Agencies Involved in International Activities* (Washington, D.C.: United States Government Printing Office, 1963).

Among the most munificent and far-flung of these programs are those of the scientists. About 15,000–20,000 scientists attend 2,000 international meetings each year. The Department of State has now established an Office of International Scientific and Technological Affairs.[31]

At the advanced level, the National Science Foundation provides a number of opportunities for international educational exchange. It makes grants financing the international travel of scientists to meetings; it grants fellowships which may be used for study in foreign countries; and it supports the visits of senior foreign scientists to United States campuses under its own auspices as well as the auspices of United States scientific societies.

The National Institute of Health distributes each year extraordinary sums of money for study and research, some of which find a way to individuals and institutions abroad. NIH trains foreign students in United States universities, grants fellowships to foreign researchers for a year or more of study abroad, and finances the establishment of study centers abroad by universities in the United States. Thus, a Professor Harry M. Smith is studying Middle Eastern blood types at laboratories of the American University Hospital in Bierut under a three year grant which was extended in 1965 for three more years. Some of the monies will be spent at his laboratories at Springfield College in Massachusetts.

The Departments of the Army, Air Force and Navy employ American teachers for schools for dependents of men in the Armed Services abroad. The National Aeronautics and Space Administration sponsors study at American universities for foreign graduate students and on-the-job training for foreign technicians at NASA laboratories. The National Archives gives a training program and has a summer institute (co-sponsored by the American University) for foreign archivists. The Bureau of the Census, the Bureau of Public Roads, the Coast and Geodetic Survey, the Bureau of Labor Standards, the Internal Revenue Service, and others, in a list that seems endless, maintain one or more programs that can be characterized as international education.

---

[31] Blum, *op. cit.*, p. 116.

CHAPTER IV

Foundations and Private Agencies of International Exchange

Of the three American sectors most heavily involved in international education and exchange—the government, the universities, and the private agencies—it is the latter that has been consistently ahead of the others, not in terms of volume of support nor in performance of services but in pioneering of experiments and programs. The private agencies have set a pace for the others and have stimulated them to function more effectively.

This chapter will review the role of the foundations, and examine programs of the major private agencies, many of which have been founded or assisted by foundation grants and perform important services to exchange scholars, universities, and the government.

The Unique Role of the American Foundations

It would be difficult to overestimate the impact of the American foundations on international education. These nonprofit, charitable institutions, endowed with the surplus funds of an affluent society, have become, in certain cases, uniquely international institutions in themselves.

There are about 15,000 foundations in the United States with assets of approximately $14.5 billion, making grants of some $800 million a year. In the American economy, their resources are not large, yet their contribution to international education has been far out of proportion to the resources involved. These foundations can operate in a unique position of freedom which allows them opportunities to tackle the "longer range, more difficult, and often controversial questions which face the nation and the world."[1] They also have examples to follow—those set by the great foundations created

---

[1] F. Emerson Andrews, ed., *Foundations, 20 View Points* (New York: Russell Sage Foundation, 1965), p. 6.

in the name of Rockefeller, of Carnegie, and more recently, of Ford.

In 1963 the Rockefeller Foundation completed a half century of activity which had been directed toward "the well-being of mankind throughout the world"—as its charter defined its purpose. For over 50 years this great institution has been the vanguard of promoting human progress around the globe. The Rockefeller Foundation pioneered in public health programs, leading the way to the conquest of malaria, hookworm, and yellow fever. Rockefeller sent agricultural specialists to aid some Latin American countries in converting agricultural deficits to surpluses. The Foundation has strengthened educational institutions both in the United States and overseas; it has supported innumerable international projects and given financial aid to gifted scholars in international exchange.

Long before World War I Andrew Carnegie made gifts to Scottish universities, thereby setting a pattern in American support of universities abroad. Since then the Carnegie Endowment and the Carnegie Corporation have continued to pioneer projects in every phase of international education.

Foundations are helping fill some of the gaps left by the government or by the universities, often extending grants in areas (geographic or educational) which are not covered by government programs. Ford and Rockefeller have made grants allowing university projects to continue abroad after government support to these projects terminated but before the usefulness of the project itself ended.

Another important role foundations have played has been in organizing and supporting research in those fields of international education which has led to better coordination and to improved government and university policies and programs. Most of the studies of international education and exchange referred to in this book, including that of the Assistant Secretary of State for Cultural Affairs, Charles Frankel, were made possible by foundation grants.

Among the scholarly studies supported by Carnegie Corporation in 1965, the annual report lists "studies of the American educational scene; studies to enhance understanding of United States relations with other areas of the world; and studies of developing countries, *with particular emphasis on the role of education*" (italics added).[2]

---

[2] *Annual Report 1965* (New York: The Carnegie Corporation, 1965).

For many years Carnegie has given substantial support to the development of area study centers such as the Russian Research Center at Harvard University.

In this brief volume, it is not possible to list completely the programs of even the major foundations. However, the work of the Ford Foundation must be mentioned. Here the programs range across the entire field of international education. They include Foreign Area Fellowships; support for studies of non-western cultures in universities (a program pioneered by Rockefeller in the 1930's); and they support manpower being trained as assistants in the economic and social development programs of newly independent countries. The Ford Foundation has an International Training and Research Program encompassing many aspects of international education and within which are offered many opportunities for students, teachers and faculty members both here and abroad.

> By the end of 1965, the Foundation had made grants for these purposes totaling $206 million. The grants have financed some forty-four foreign-area programs; assisted twenty-four universities in placing graduate international studies programs on a permanent, competitive basis with other academic subjects; and helped more than 135 liberal arts colleges bring teaching on Asia, Africa, and Latin America into regular academic programs.[3]

Though small in comparison with that of government, foundations' support for teacher and student exchange has been most effective. All the large foundations (and many of the smaller ones) have programs which either directly or indirectly support international exchange of teachers and scholars at various levels.

Although relatively few foundations have *specialized* in international educational exchange, the bulk of what has been done has been done by the largest of the private foundations in the United States. In monetary terms, The Ford Foundation is probably the most substantial agent in the field; although historically, The Rockefeller Foundation and the Carnegie Corporation of New York have set the pace.

The Rockefeller report from the third quarter of 1965 listed 156 fellows and scholars from twenty-nine countries whose awards be-

---

[3] The Ford Foundation, *Context the World* (New York: The Foundation, February 1966), p. 4. This is one of a series of booklets on activities supported by the Ford Foundation.

came active in that quarter. Seventy of these fellowships were in agricultural sciences, fifty-nine were in the humanities and social sciences and twenty-seven were in the medical and natural sciences.

The Carnegie Endowment for International Peace has made its most significant contributions at a very high level of international educational exchange, sponsoring research and study of international problems, particularly in the fields of international law, international economics, international organizations.

The Endowment maintains an outstanding Hospitality Information Service for the United Nations in New York. The Service is a clearinghouse for information about the services provided by non-governmental organizations in the United States to missions and delegations to the United Nations. It also maintains the handsome Carnegie International Center, opened in 1953, to serve as headquarters not only for the Carnegie Endowment but also for non-profit organizations concerned with international affairs, human welfare, and civic and cultural activities. This Center houses the permanent offices of more than thirty organizations, the largest number of which are involved in one way or another with international educational exchange. For example, the African-American Institute is located in the Center, as are the American-Korean Foundation, the Association of International Relations Clubs, the Governmental Affairs Institute, the Information Center for American Travelers to the Soviet Union, and many others.

The Carnegie Endowment also supports the Foreign Policy Association, a non-partisan organization for citizen education in international affairs, which operates a World Affairs Center and World Affairs Book Center on the first floor of the building.

Finally it must be mentioned that the new Education and World Affairs receives support from the Carnegie Corporation.

At the international symposia, institutes, and in the publications sponsored by the Endowment, it is working at the cutting edge of international relations and, almost incidentally, supporting international scholarly exchange at a very high level.

Outside of the "giants" among foundations supporting international education, there are a number of private foundations pursuing less spectacular but vital programs in this field. Frequently such support takes the form of specific scholarships to students and educators from abroad.

This brief discussion can only be a superficial overview of the foundations' important role. It must be added, however, that this role too, especially in relation to the government programs and university programs in international exchange, is in need of careful re-examination.

By no means are all 15,000 American foundations interested in international education. The student or teacher seeking support for an overseas study would do well to consult *The Foundation Directory*, second edition, which has a summary of international educational efforts. The directory itself is supported by the Russell Sage Foundation and is produced by the Foundation Library Center directed by F. Emerson Andrews. The address is 444 Madison Avenue, New York, New York. Further information on foundations can be obtained at the Center and at various smaller foundation library centers in other parts of the country.

Applications for foundation grants must usually be made well in advance of the period for which support is requested, and preparing the applications themselves involves quite a lot of time and skill. Those seeking a foundation grant will save time, and quite possibly some disappointment, by studying the excellent informational literature that foundations make available on direct request, or which can be found throughout the country at universities and especially at foundation library centers.

International Programs of Special Agencies

The important part played by private organizations in international educational exchange seems in little danger of diminishing despite the federal government's increased involvement. Before World War II, private organizations were ahead of the government as far as interest and activity in international programs was concerned; the government has caught up here. But these private organizations still perform unique and vital functions that government has not been able to do.

The patriarch of the private organizations is the Institute of International Education (IIE) which, like other private organizations, developed in direct response to the desire for international study abroad, and out of the need for particular services. The long-standing services of the Conference Board of Associated Research Councils and the newer activities of Education and World Affairs have made equally important contributions in this field. A number of private organizations—such as the African-American Institute, the Asia Society, and the Japan Society—have a regional and cultural orientation which by their very nature can offer superior resources and services on the inter-cultural level. A number of other private organizations, including the Committee on International Relations of the American Association of Colleges of Teacher Education, have educational programs with a professional slant.

Another group of organizations developed to meet particular needs: this group includes such blue-ribbon organizations as the Experiment in International Living; the Council on Student Travel and Educational Travel, Incorporated of the United States National Student Association. These are geared to assisting the foreign students by (1) providing travel arrangements, (2) helping in the orientation procedure, (3) providing hospitality facilities and services of a host country, and the like.

For every organization mentioned in this chapter, there are numerous others whose functions are similar to the prototypes discussed here and whose activities can be found by referring to any of a number of excellent directories available for this purpose.

Institute for International Education (IIE)

A review of the private organizations facilitating international educational exchange logically begins with a summary of the multifaceted services of the Institute of International Education. This was one of the first organizations in the United States directed toward the international extension of education. For nearly half a century IIE handled the administration of public and private grants for study abroad, and served the needs of foreign students in the United States.

Students from the United States planning to study abroad will find that IIE handles the preliminary screening of applications for government grants under the Fulbright-Hays Act of 1961. In addition, students interested in studying in Poland or Rumania will discover that IIE takes care of the administration of grants sponsored jointly by the United States and these Eastern European countries. Students interested in Latin America, who apply for grants administered jointly by the United States government and Latin American governments under the Inter-American Cultural Convention, can apply through IIE. Many of the grants offered by other foreign governments are also handled by IIE—so are the growing number of grants for study abroad offered by our country's private businesses. Regional offices for IIE are located in Chicago, Denver, Houston, San Francisco, and Washington, D.C. They will assist the American student in his exploration of avenues for study abroad.

Foreign students wishing to study in the United States make the acquaintance of IIE early in their search for a school, and renew the relationship several times along the way. IIE has consultants in 24 countries, and has offices abroad in Lima, Peru; Bangkok, Thailand; Nairobi, Kenya; and Paris, France. These offices interview students who wish to study in the United States but who have no sponsor. They transmit to institutions in the United States information about credits earned by foreign students; they direct foreign students to whatever schools and grants will fulfil their needs. There are offices of IIE in New York City where applications of many a students from abroad are processed. The applications handled here may be made by the student for study under one of several auspices: the federal government, any of a number of foundations, or UNESCO.

If the foreign student does get to the United States, his travel arrangements may be arranged for by IIE. He may attend a summer orientation program administered by IIE at certain college campuses or at the headquarters of the Experiment in International Living in Putney, Vermont. Once settled on a campus, he can get in touch with one of the regional offices of IIE for help; or he may find a member of the staff of one of these regional offices visiting his campus to check up on his program and needs.

In recent years IIE has added to its former services: (1) by taking care of East Africans who came to the United States in the early 1960's, (2) by administering the Council on Higher Education in the American Republics known as CHEAR (which was formed to initiate and implement cooperative programs of education in the Western Hemisphere), (3) by supervising a program entitled Training Opportunities for Youth Leaders (TOYL) (which is financed by government funds and which provides summer programs as well as supplementary funds in an attempt to accelerate and intensify the studies of self-sponsored students).

To broaden opportunities for sponsored study in the United States, the Council on Graduate Schools–IIE Cooperative Fellowship Program places students in schools belonging to the Council. These schools provide tuition; the government underwrites living expenses; and travel expenses are assumed by Braniff International Airways. IIE also performs services for short term visitors coming to the United States, and for those going abroad under government and private auspices. It assists with the preparation of itineraries, helps make professional appointments, and arranges hospitality programs.

The Institute of International Education provides invaluable help through its many publications, which index and analyze programs for international educational exchange. Among the most useful are the *Handbooks for International Study*.[4] One edition, being for Foreign Nationals, contains information about national and regional organizations in the United States offering help to foreign nationals, and it lists committees, bi-national centers, educational commissions, and organizations abroad which offer services to foreign nationals wishing to study in the United States. The companion volume, for United States Nationals, provides equally useful information about study programs, and about organizations here and abroad which assist Americans studying overseas. Each publication contains an extensive bibliography. It issues numerous other helpful publications, such as *English Language and Orientation Programs in the United States, Educational Exchange Within the Atlantic Area*, and *IIE Survey of the African Student: His Achievements and His Problems*.[5]

Conference Board of Associated Research Councils

Another private organization performing work under contract to the federal government, with a long history of service to international educational exchange, is the Committee on International Exchange of Persons of the Conference Board of Associated Research Councils. The Conference Board is the coordinating body for four major professional organizations of the academic world— the National Research Council, the American Council of Learned

---

4 Institute of International Education, *Handbook of International Study: For U.S. Nationals* and *Handbook of International Study: For Foreign Nationals* (New York: The Institute, 1965).

5 Published by the Institute of International Education, New York.

Societies, the Social Science Research Council, and the American Council on Education. It was formed in 1946. A major objective is the promoting of international cooperation in education. Shortly after the passage of the Fulbright Amendment, the Board of Foreign Scholarships of the Department of State requested the Conference Board administer a grant program for post-doctoral or post-professional applicants. The Committee on International Exchange of Persons, then created, now has a full-time executive secretary, a full-time staff and forty subcommittees trained to screen applications for the grants offered. In addition, the Committee's duties include making a preliminary selection of Americans who want to lecture abroad and supervising the exchange programs of foreign research scholars and lecturers coming to the United States.

The member groups of the Conference Board have their own programs in international education. For example, the American Council of Learned Societies offers many fellowships for study abroad—particularly for Asian, Slavic, and East European area studies. The Social Science Research Council sponsors fellowships abroad for major area study programs in Africa, Latin America, the Middle East, and for studies on contemporary China.

American Association of Colleges for Teacher Education (AACTE)

Another professional organization of particular interest is the American Association of Colleges for Teacher Education. Its Committee on International Relations actively promotes an expanded program of study abroad. It encourages its members to provide scholarships. With the Department of State, it conducts the Inter-Institutional Affiliation Project through which colleges in the United States exchange information about education programs with institutions in various parts of the world in order to encourage the exchange of students and faculty. Each year at its February meeting it is host to foreign teachers who are in the United States under programs of the United States Office of Education.

Of special value is its directory, the *AACTE Handbook of International Education Programs,*[6] which lists overseas opportunities for

---

[6] American Association of Colleges of Teacher Education, *AACTE Handbook of International Education Programs,* H. Kenneth Barber, ed. (Washington, D.C.: The Association, 1963).

students, professors, and administrators—particularly on the doctoral and post-doctoral level. It also lists professional opportunities for teaching abroad. Another section of the directory lists private organizations which support active programs in international affairs and education, while a final list contains the names and addresses of individuals in the embassies who can be contacted for information about opportunities available in specific countries.

American Council on Education

The American Council on Education also has a special apparatus for international education—the Commission on International Education. This organ consults with American colleges and the federal government in their development of programs of international education; acts as liaison between the government and the academic community; publishes valuable studies on international education including the periodical, *Bulletin on International Education.* The latter surveys federal, academic, foundation, and other private activities engaged in international education.

Education and World Affairs (EWA)

Education and World Affairs is a unique organization, a direct answer to the need voiced by the Committee on the University and World Affairs, which published the influential report *The University and World Affairs* in 1960.[7] Funded by the Ford Foundation and the Carnegie Corporation of New York, the focus of Education and World Affairs is exclusively on expanding the international dimension of education in the United States. This objective led to EWA's publication of a number of studies probing the extent and quality of international programs. These excellent publications are:

> *The College and World Affairs*
> *AID and the Universities*
> *The United States Office of Education: An International Dimension*

---

[7] *The University and World Affairs* (New York: The Ford Foundation, 1960). Also known as the Morrill Report after the chairman, J. L. Morrill. Other important members of the Committee were Dean Rusk, John Gardner and Senator William Fulbright.

The Foreign Student, Whom Shall We Welcome?
(a well written and terse analysis of the foreign student problems in the United States)

The Overseas Selection of Foreign Students

The University Looks Abroad: Case Studies of the International Programs of Six Universities—Michigan State, Wisconsin, Tulane, Stanford, Indiana

International Education Program 1966

This last title was published in March 1966. As a text and brief appraisal of the bill introduced in the House of Representatives for an International and Health Education Act, this handy informative publication exemplifies the excellent information service which EWA renders to the whole range of institutions and persons interested in international education. The directory, *Intercultural Education*, published under EWA sponsorship, lists fellowship opportunities open to teachers and students who are *not* area and language specialists but who have a declared interest in learning about neglected areas of the world. This directory also lists forthcoming conferences of disciplinary, inter-disciplinary, and area study associations. In addition it contains a selected bibliography referring to other source materials.

EWA administers two rather unique and valuable overseas programs: (1) its Overseas Educational Service assists United States teachers and professors abroad and acts as an intermediary for teachers who wish to teach abroad, and (2) its University Service Center in Hong Kong assists the many scholars working on research projects in the Far East.

African-American Institute

The African-American Institute was set up to assist Africans in receiving an education in the United States with the idea that their responsibility was to return to their native land and help in its development. This theory is implemented imaginatively. The African-American Institute administers 20 educational programs in 30 African countries. Many of these programs provide for the education of Africans in the United States, but all programs are directed toward the growth of African education. As educational systems become established in these native countries, the emphasis will shift to African universities where educational leadership will be developed. Through the African Scholarship Program of American Universities (ASPAU), qualified African undergraduates, after rigid selection in cooperation with educational and government authorities in sub-Saharan Africa, study at leading colleges and universities in the United States. The financial costs are shared by the African governments, which underwrite travel costs; the Agency for International Development, which takes care of living costs; and the participating universities, foundations, and the African-American Institute, which handle the other fees. The Educational Testing Service, the United Negro College Fund, and the Council on Student Travel also assist with the administration of the program. Indicative of its standards is the fact that 300 Africans are selected each year after 10,000 applicants are screened, tested, and interviewed.

Another program of the African-American Institute is the African Graduate Fellowship Program, which offers 50 fellowships annually through the support of AID and 20 through the funds of the Department of State and UNESCO, in cooperation with the Council on Graduate Schools. There are special programs for students from Guinea and Kenya for short term programs, and others for African women in the United States.

The African-American Institute publishes *Africa Reports.* In other activities it assists with the programming of leaders, specialists, and individuals receiving educational travel grants from the Department of State. It did have an active teacher placement program for American teachers in Africa, but this has given way to the Peace Corps program (except for the continuation of the Teachers for West Africa Program of Elizabethtown College which sends about 30 teachers to Africa each year). The African-American Institute is in the forefront of new efforts being made for the educational development of the "third world," which is of crucial importance in Africa.

National Association for Foreign Student Affairs (NAFSA)

Another private organization which serves a unique purpose in international educational exchange is the National Association for Foreign Student Affairs. This is a professional membership association of foreign student advisers—those who teach English as a foreign language, Fulbright program advisers and other persons and institutions concerned with foreign students in the United States. NAFSA, with offices at 809 United Nations Plaza, New York, New York 10017, assists its members in helping meet the needs of visiting students, faculty, and distinguished guests. It publishes valuable studies and bibliographies, a handbook for foreign student advisers, and occasional papers on English language teaching.

The Experiment in International Living

It is axiomatic that much of education occurs outside the classroom. Several private organizations have established themselves to help this major, extra-curricular area of the educational experience of those who are abroad. The Experiment in International Living emphasizes the mutual value of individual contact with the families abroad. To carry this out, the Experiment arranges to have students and others live abroad with a family in their home; to travel, study, and work with them, frequently in inter-cultural groups. It also sets up homestays for foreign students in the United States preceding their attendance at one of our colleges or universities; it conducts orientation sessions for foreign students at its headquarters in Putney, Vermont; and it has undertaken a number of Peace Corps training programs for the government.

Recently, the Experiment undertook the administration of Latin American Programs of American Universities (LASPAU) which is modeled on the program of the African American Institute for African students (ASPAU). The program will begin by selecting students from three universities in Colombia. These students will take a summer orientation session at the headquarters of the Experiment at Putney; this will be followed by four years of schooling in the United States. The final semester of study will be at a university in Colombia. Following a program pattern similar to the African-American Institute in which the foreign student is educated in the United States and then returns to his native country with the responsibility of helping in its development, this program is focused in the direction of eventually establishing a sound educational system in Latin America. The United States government is also looking in this direction as it becomes less concerned with educational exchange in the Atlantic area.

Council on Student Travel

The Council on Student Travel, Inc., 777 United Nations Plaza, New York, New York 10017, evolved at the end of World War II to facilitate resumption of student travel overseas. Originally concerned only with arranging charter trips on United States government ships, and later on private lines, the Council has developed broader programs including the overseas plans of many students travelling abroad from the United States. Its broadened scope includes the sponsorship of conferences and workshops (most recently in Paris, Tokyo, Philadelphia, and San Francisco); the arrangements for overseas passage, by both ship and air, for groups sponsored by member organizations; shipboard orientation programs; and an information service. The Council on Student Travel has offices in Tokyo and Paris. It does some programming for visits abroad, and sponsors a special program for Japanese students in the United States. Its publications (unusually handsome) include directories of academic programs abroad for college and high school students, and a *Guide to Institutional Self-Study and Evaluation of Educational Programs Abroad*. The growth of the Council on Student Travel and its needed expansion into substantive areas is an interesting reflection of the tremendous growth of interest and activity in the area of international education.

Programs of similar direction are found under the auspices of Educational Travel Incorporated of the United States National Student Association, 265 Madison Avenue, New York, New York 10016. For nearly two decades this office has been advising students about their travel arrangements. Unique is its relationship with the national student unions of other countries, including Poland and the Soviet Union, which allows it to arrange a number of exchange programs, including one of the few to the Soviet Union and Eastern Europe. It publishes a directory entitled *Work, Study, Travel Abroad* which gives travel and tour advice; lists national student travel organizations; and arranges tours (including a study tour in France, an Italian art tour, a politics and economics study tour of the European regional organizations and United Nations agencies in Europe).

Consultative Service on United States
Undergraduate Study Abroad

One of the newest organizations serving international education is also one of the most important. The Consultative Service on United States Undergraduate Study Abroad is a coordinating venture of the Association of American Colleges, the Council on Student Travel, the Experiment in International Living, and the Institute of International Education. It was formed in the spring of 1963 with a grant by the Carnegie Corporation of New York. Its objectives are: (1) to secure full and precise information on international education, (2) to coordinate the rapidly proliferating ventures of United States educational institutions for undergraduate study abroad, (3) to ease communication and cooperation between these institutions, and (4) to establish the basis for determining standards which will evaluate undergraduate study abroad programs. Under the direction of Stephen Freeman, formerly President of Middlebury College, it has published the definitive directory of undergraduate study-abroad programs—lists of academic year programs by region, and lists of the many independent study and summer programs.[8]

Operation Crossroads Africa, 150 Fifth Avenue, New York, New York, is an exciting example of an organization involved in summer work programs. This program sends students from the United States to Africa to work on construction projects, to assist teacher training and to be medical assistants. The effectiveness of Crossroads Africa was a major influence leading to the establishment of the United States Peace Corps. In 1964 a "reverse flow" pilot project sent a number of African youth leaders to the United States for 45 days in a leadership training program here.

Several organizations are meeting the need for a clearing house to arrange jobs for the many students who wish to gain an overseas experience through working abroad. The International Association of Students in the Economic and Commercial Sciences, 51 East 42nd Street, New York, is such an organization. It is international but has a United States member group. Jobs are exchanged on a one-for-one basis. Students of a member institution receive as many

---

[8] Institute of International Education: *Undergraduate Study Abroad,* Report of the Consulate Service on U.S. Undergraduate Study Abroad (New York: The Institute, 1964).

jobs abroad as they can provide for foreign students in the United States.

A brief note should be made of sources of information for high school students wishing to study or visit abroad. The American Field Service is preeminent in this field. Among other private agencies promoting student exchange are the National Catholic Welfare Conference, 1312 Massachusetts Avenue, N.W., Washington, D.C., and the International Christian Youth Exchange, 475 Riverside Drive, New York 27, New York, to mention only two of many church organizations which are assisting in this field. Many other national organizations handle arrangements for foreign students to attend high school in the United States.

International Business

A growing number of businesses are entering the field of international educational exchange. Their international divisions offer yet another source of funds and programming established to meet the growing demand for an education abroad. For example, American Overseas Petroleum, Ltd. has a scholarship program for six students from Indonesia, Turkey, and Libya to study in the United States. Sankei Scholarships have been established recently by Chigio Mizuno, a Japanese industrialist, for twenty Japanese undergraduates to study in the United States. This program began in September of 1965. Xerox sponsored a Xerox International Fellowship for Mexico as of 1965–1966. In 1965 Braniff International Airways, Pan American Grace Airways, and Pan American Airways supplied funds to offset the living expenses of foreign graduate students in the United States, in cooperation with a program of the Institute for International Education and the Council of Graduate Schools. Last year more than thirty firms gave unrestricted grants to the Institute for International Education while others continued to support already established programs for scholarships from abroad.

Community Agencies

A final category of private agencies interested in international education must be mentioned to conclude this survey—the community organization. There are uncountable organizations in almost every city in the United States that serve foreign visitors in their community. In *The Fulbright Program,* Walter Johnson and Francis Colligan describe in detail many of these programs.[9]

The National Council for Community Services to International Visitors (COSERV) is one of a complex of organizations stemming from the Meridian House, 1630 Crescent Avenue, N.W. in Washington, D.C. COSERV coordinates many of the activities of many community organizations and serves as a liaison between these groups and the Department of State. It publishes a directory to community organizations and a *Handbook for Travelers to the United States,* in English, French, and Spanish. There are a number of other directories to community organizations willing and often eager to welcome foreign students. Such a listing can be found in the Institute of International Education's *Handbook of International Study for Foreign Nationals.*

What significant services do these organizations offer? In the impersonal world of large cities and universities, they may offer the only opportunity for foreign students to experience the warmth of an American home. Conversely, the effect on the American family can be enormous. An evening's discussion with one student from Ghana may do more to arouse interest and concern in international affairs than years of blazing headlines.

This survey has only skimmed the surface in revealing the vast numbers of private organizations there are in the United States whose purpose is to further international educational exchange. In addition to the directories already cited, individuals wishing to probe more deeply may consult the volume of the Council on Foreign Relations entitled *American Agencies Interested in International Affairs*[10] which lists many of the private groups and which has an index by subject. The Technical Assistance Information Clearing House publishes *U.S. Non-Profit Organizations, Volunteer Agencies, Missions and Foundations Participating in Technical Assistance Abroad: A Directory*[11] while *Intercom* magazine published an issue in January 1963 devoted to a "Directory of Voluntary Organizations in World Affairs." Two sound and helpful directories with a

---

[9] Walter Johnson and Francis J. Colligan, *The Fulbright Program, A History* (Chicago: University of Chicago Press, 1965).

[10] Compiled by Donald Wasson (New York: Praeger, 1964).

[11] (New York: Manhattan Printing Company, 1964).

regional orientation are *American Institutions and Organizations Interested in Asia, A Reference Directory*[12] published by The Asia Society and *African Programs of U.S. Organizations.*[13]

---

[12] (New York: Laplinger Publishing Co., Inc., 1961).

[13] United States Department of State, External Research Staff, Bureau of Intelligence and Research, *African Programs of U.S. Organizations, A Selective Directory* (Washington, D.C.: U.S. Government Printing Office, 1965).

CHAPTER V

Programs of American Colleges
and Universities

> The academic estate has for centuries engaged more than most other elements of society in international communication of scholarship and ideas.[1]

In this chapter the role of the American universities and colleges in international exchange will be discussed. A few examples of the international programs of universities and colleges in the United States, great and small, and their study-abroad programs for foreign students and for American students will be cited. Though there are some opportunities for exchange and study-abroad for teachers and students preparing to teach, this field has a relatively small percentage of all international exchange programs. In 1962, only 2 per cent of study-abroad programs were in the field of education. Almost as many professors go abroad in one year as teachers have gone in 15 years.[2] This has improved with the Teachers for Africa program of Columbia University and the Peace Corps. It should continue to improve with the greater emphasis of the American Association of Colleges of Teacher Education and the government programs on programs for teachers.

William Marvel, in his introduction to *The University Looks Abroad,* speaks of the growing "alikeness" of universities around the world and suggests there will be ". . . strengthening of the *international intellectual community.*" The universities are the institutional form of this intellectual community which translate it "from concept to reality."[3]

The American colleges and universities are not only members of

---

[1] Edward W. Weidner, *The World Role of Universities* (New York, McGraw-Hill Book Company, Inc., 1962), p. 2.

[2] R. Freeman Butts, *American Education in International Development* (New York: Harper & Row, Publishers, 1963), pp. 13–14.

[3] William Marvel, ed., *The University Looks Abroad* (New York: Education and World Affairs, 1966), pp. xii–xiii.

this community but, since World War II, have taken a leading role in promoting it. For the most part in the past, American universities have "drifted on the seas of international exchange programs without rudder and direction, without compass and destination. Most university programs have been improvisations, lacking a fundamental philosophy or relevance to the university and its objectives."[4] Much the same might be said for the early government programs. In the early 1960's, however, after two decades of development, the American universities have become one of the prime movers in international education. Certain large universities, such as Michigan State University, have been the pathfinders in international education, although many smaller colleges have developed some kind of international program.

In fact, a majority of the two thousand institutions of higher learning in the United States participate in international educational exchange in one or more of its aspects: (1) by accepting foreign students, (2) by sending students abroad, (3) by including international courses in the curriculum, or (4) by technical assistance programs, usually under government contract, which include the exchange of teachers and technicians.

The international outreach of American colleges has enriched educational experience. Increasing numbers of prospective students and parents, when choosing a college to attend, look for this international aspect in a college program. As a result, few colleges can afford to ignore it or do without it. The responsibility of the universities in world affairs is in the best university tradition. It is no less than that of "enlarging our horizons as a free society" helping "to educate the leaders and help build the educational foundations of newer nations and to cooperate with educational institutions in other nations in order to help create a free international society."[5]

The situation which Dr. Weidner described as drifting has improved, but there is much room for further progress. The record of the United States colleges and universities is uneven. Leading institutions have developed positive policies: (1) by having international centers with a director, dean, or vice president assuming responsibility for all the university's activities in the international field, (2) by appointing deans of international programs to act as college-wide

---

[4] Weidner, *op. cit.,* p. 288.
[5] Report of the Committee on the University and World Affairs, *The University and World Affairs* (New York: The Ford Foundation, 1960), p. 2.

coordinators, (3) by having international activities and programs handled by association administrators of a group of cooperating colleges, and (4) by having a Foreign Student Adviser on campus to coordinate international activities. The Foreign Student Adviser may or may not be a part of the teaching program at his institution.[6]

In the uninhibited proliferation of international studies and study abroad sponsored by United States colleges and universities, many types of programs have developed. Although broad similarities exist among the overseas programs of liberal arts colleges, no two programs are identical. Although the institutionalization of arrangements for the foreign student on the United States campus has proceeded along similar lines on each campus, the complexity or simplicity of the foreign student office and its synchronization with administration varies. Perhaps, however, a brief description of the international programs of several large universities, a liberal arts college, and a teacher training institution will give the reader an idea of the kinds of programs colleges and universities in the United States offer. They will serve as rough prototypes. Sources for further information about the programs of colleges and universities will be included.

Perhaps the most extensive, and at the same time least coordinated, programs for foreign and United States students exist on the campuses of the large universities. In the past few years, tremendous gains have been made in coordinating these programs—with procedures which have been of necessity innovative, and fortunately imaginative. Stanford University and Michigan State University have arrived at fundamentally different solutions. Each serves as a valid sample of many other programs in the United States.

Stanford University

In 1906 Stanford initiated the first course in Far Eastern history taught anywhere in the United States.[7] This was only the beginning

---

[6] For a detailed analysis of the foreign student advisor, *see* Homer D. Higbee, *The Status of Foreign Student Advising in United States Universities and Colleges* (East Lansing: Michigan State University Institute of Research on Overseas Programs, 1961).

[7] Education and World Affairs, *The University Looks Abroad to World Affairs at Six American Universities* (New York: Walker and Company, 1965), p. 6. The information in this section on Stanford and Michigan State is based on this readable and informative study.

of a half-century of interest in world affairs and of the education of foreign students on its campus and of its students abroad. Stanford ranks nineteenth in the numbers game (percentage of foreign students to total enrollment) with a very high percentage of its foreign students, about 88 per cent, enrolled on the graduate level. On the other side of the exchange coin, it is interesting to note that Stanford ranks first in the number of Peace Corps volunteers per capita in its student body, third in the number of Marshall Scholarships received when compared with all other United States colleges and universities, and among the top ten in the number of Rhodes scholarships received by its students compared to other colleges and universities in the United States. Another gauge of its international involvement is the nearly 50 per cent of its student body who have had overseas experience, and the 20 per cent of its students who are involved in international programs of one sort or another.[8]

The administration has established the position of Assistant Graduate Dean for International Students on the Stanford campus. Thus it is first among a number of schools moving beyond the Foreign Student Adviser machinery to a more institutionalized arrangement. This title brings with it prestige and means that more influence can be exerted on campuses on behalf of the needs of its foreign students. There is also an office of Foreign Graduate Admissions which coordinates the foreign student admissions procedures of the many departments involved. The Bechtel International Student Center is used primarily by foreign students and United States students who have been abroad; it houses the offices of its foreign student administrators and the Community Committee for International Students (which arranges hospitality for foreign students). Unlike some institutions, Stanford requires, and provides, remedial English courses for some of its foreign students. It considers these courses highly popular, successful, and justified.

The study-abroad programs of Stanford are the "island type"—in other words self-sufficient "little Stanfords" abroad. This arrangement allows sophomores at Stanford to go abroad, permitting preprofessional students, who couldn't go after their sophomore year, to go abroad. Foreign universities will usually not accept American students below the junior year level, but the Stanford "islands" per-

---

[8] *Ibid.*, p. 7.

mit this. The study-abroad campuses are located in Stuttgart, Germany; in Tours, France; and, in Florence, Italy. In 1965–1966, two new study centers were established—at Harlaxton Manor, one hundred miles north of London and at Semmering, Austria, near Vienna. Students at these "island centers" need not necessarily have highly proficient language abilities. They pay the same tuition and expenses as they would if attending the Stanford campus in California. "Islands" allow a four day study week which encourages travel. Twice a year, 400 Stanford students enroll in these five centers for a six month period. Some results: (1) an increased interest in international affairs, (2) more students majoring in history, language, art, and art history, (3) pressures for faculty in California to live in the dormitories of Stanford in order to approximate more closely the student-faculty relationships held at the overseas study centers, (4) agitation for coeducational housing, and (5) demands for certain overseas customs such as serving wine at meals.[9]

In addition to these study centers, there are a number of other Stanford programs for study abroad, among them the Stanford-Warsaw University Graduate Student Exchange program and a program of the Modern Language Department in cooperation with NDEA, which sends about 80 American teachers to a site near Stuttgart, Germany for language training and teacher training each summer.

Of particular interest is the Stanford Comparative Education Center, part of the School of Education, which has established a doctoral program for individuals holding a master's degree in some substantive discipline and two years successful employment in education in either the United States or overseas. The students in the comparative education degree program—of whom 60 per cent are United States students and 40 per cent are foreign students—undertake a three year program, one of which is spent on a research program overseas.

The international facets of Stanford University are located rather autonomously in its many departments. This loosely federated approach is very extensive in its scope and influence. It is coordinated

---

[9] William Marvel, ed., *The University Looks Abroad, loc. cit.,* pp. 13–15.

by a Committee on International Studies, recently established to review and analyze the university's role in international studies.

Michigan State University

A near opposite of the Stanford University approach is found at Michigan State University, which has institutionalized its international programs to an unusual degree. Its rather unique structure, which may be imitated increasingly on other campuses, and its involvement in technical assistance programs throughout the world, are perhaps the hallmarks of its international educational set-up. *The University Looks Abroad* rejects the criticism made that Michigan State University has been over-eager internationally in order to gain its prestige by "hopping on the bandwagon" of government contracts abroad. The fact is that more than any other university in the United States, Michigan State University has made a determined effort to intensify its relationships abroad and to increase the feedback of these relationships to its campus in Michigan. By doing this, it has added substantial international dimension to its program.

In 1951 Michigan State began its present program of cooperation with the University of the Ryukyus for the Department of the Army; in 1953 it developed a program in Sao Paolo, Brazil under government auspices; and in 1960 it signed a government contract for work in Nigeria, which led to the establishment of the University of Nigeria on the model of the United States land grant college pattern. In addition, a summer exchange program developed exchanging about thirty Michigan State students for twenty students from the University of Nigeria each year.

To handle its international programs, Michigan State established an Office of International Programs which is directed by an Assistant Dean of International Programs, an Associate Dean, three Assistant Deans (for research, exchange programs, and overseas operations), an Assistant to the Dean of Administration, and an Educational Exchange Adviser, replacing the Foreign Student Adviser.

Michigan State University ranks fifteenth in the United States in the percentage of foreign students to its total enrollment, 60 per cent of which are enrolled at the graduate level. They are served by a Counselling Center, special orientation programs, a newsletter, and an English Languages Training Center. In addition to their regular studies, foreign students serve as a resource in an extra-mural professional growth and development program for high school and elementary teachers and for teacher workshops in the state of Michigan.

Michigan State University has no junior year abroad programs for its students. It does have an International Doctoral Fellowship Program for professors doing overseas research, and it has a cooperative set-up with European Language and Education Centers, which allows Michigan State professors and students to live in the centers in Cologne, Lisbon, and Madrid for the summer.

Through a most unusual arrangement, Peace Corps volunteers can work for a graduate degree and can qualify for State of Michigan secondary teacher certification while carrying out their Peace Corps assignment in Nigeria. The Peace Corps Volunteers do independent study, supervised teaching, and seminar work under the direction of Michigan State faculty members in Nigeria. This work is completed after a final term at Michigan State—at which time they supplement the Michigan State teaching faculty.

Yale University

Yale University has carried the idea of an overseas experience as an integral part of the student's curriculum a further step along in its pilot program for 1966–1967 which offers a one year work program abroad. Financed by a grant from the Carnegie Corporation, in the 1966–1967 academic year, twelve Yale students who have completed their sophomore year will go to twelve countries for a year of work and study on projects of their own design. For example, one of these students will work with ACCION, the community development program in Venezuela; another will work at the Schweitzer Hospital in Lambarane, Africa; still others will teach in schools in Okayama, Japan, in Ajmer, India and in Zaria, Nigeria. At the same time these students will be working on study projects which they have designed. They will make regular reports on these study projects to their home campus. Prior to their departure and after their return, these Yale students will receive instruction geared to their experiences overseas and intensive counseling will be given. They will also have the privilege of returning to the Yale campus over a period of ten years after they graduate, during which time they can review or deepen their knowledge on their project.

They can return whenever they wish and stay as long as they wish.

The Yale program is deliberately planned to break up the four-year academic experiences of students by immersing them in practical activity. This is done with the hope of stimulating their interests, developing their maturity, and making the Bachelor of Arts degree a terminal degree. It is one of a number of projects that many colleges and universities in the United States are using to encourage a more realistic and valuable blending of academic theory and practice. The independence of the Yale students when they go abroad makes the Yale project unique not only for its length as a field experience but for its veering away from the increasing pattern of "island" or "peninsular" campuses abroad.

The Bologna Center of the School of Advanced International Studies of the Johns Hopkins University

A good example of an "island-type" school abroad is the Bologna Center of the School of Advanced International Studies of the Johns Hopkins University. One of the older of the programs of overseas study, the Bologna Center is the site of international studies involving an equal number of American and European students each year. Staffed by both American and European professors with English the medium of instruction, the Bologna Center is a self-contained unit in the university town of Bologna, Italy. Students live (with some exceptions) in the apartments of the Center in carefully mixed groups (an American, an Italian, a Frenchman and a Belgian, for example); European students, who usually study at the Center for one year, are frequently the recipients of grants from their governments for these studies and receive a certificate upon completion of the year. Each year, a few of the European students are awarded scholarships for an additional year, leading to the Master of Arts degree at The School of Advanced International Studies in Washington, D.C. American students must spend either the year prior or after their year in Bologna at the school in Washington in order to receive the Master of Arts degree.

A highlight of the academic year is a month-long tour of the offices of the European communities throughout Europe. European graduates have reached, in the short history of the Bologna Center, distinguished levels in the Foreign Services of their countries. American students have been given a unique opportunity to live and work with their European colleagues.

Smaller Colleges

The study-abroad programs of small liberal arts institutions are among the very best—and the very worst. Their smallness either allows a flexibility which produces the most imaginative and effective of study-abroad programs, or it means limited resources, resulting in the establishment of the most diluted and mediocre of overseas programs.

Among the more interesting variations on the theme of junior year abroad programs are the growing number of already mentioned "island" or "peninsular" campuses abroad which transplant a varying portion of the United States institution abroad while imbibing of the culture and resources of the foreign country. Fairleigh Dickinson College, whose Graduate College was installed recently in a converted abbey in Wroxton, England, is one of a number of institutions investing in facilities of their own in a foreign country and employing both American and foreign professors.

Beloit College

Beloit College in Wisconsin has established a unique program of study-abroad projects which may serve as a model to other similar-type schools. Seminar groups in 1966–1967 will study at the University of Rennes in France; Schiller College in Germany; the University of Guadalajara in Mexico; and in Taiwan under the direction of a faculty member from Beloit. Students undertake tailored studies for credit while living with private families. Then through special arrangements between Beloit and a number of foreign institutions, students enroll in the regular courses of schools in Finland, Japan, Korea, Lebanon, Greece, and Turkey. All these courses are in English. A further feature is that a number of Beloit College students go abroad for independent study each year. At Beloit, study-abroad programs are an integral part of both the international program of the College and of the innovative and flexible course of studies of the College as a whole. In 1966, 80 Beloit students were involved in programs in 13 countries.

Springfield College

Though in some respects not a typical teachers' college, Springfield College in Massachusetts (1,500 students) is preparing at least 85 per cent of its students for positions in education, the largest percentage of whom become elementary and secondary school teachers.

In the past decade, the college has pushed forward to enhance its international outreach. One approach was to have international educational experience placed high on the list of qualifications required when hiring new faculty members. Then, unlike many a university or college with far greater resources, Springfield has followed a positive program of recruitment and selection which has resulted in having an extraordinarily high caliber of students from overseas matriculate. These are mostly graduate students in physical education. Springfield's policy recognizes that foreign students at the graduate level have more to gain from and more to give to the American educational experience.

Recently Springfield College established a small "International Center" under a Foreign Student Adviser who was once a foreign student himself.

Curriculum has been a bit slow in catching up with the more "glamorous" foreign student program, and the summer programs, Peace Corps training program, Crossroads Africa, and a youth leadership project in British Guiana. The required freshman course in western civilization taught by a team of excellent instructors, however, has had its injections of content on "non-western" cultures. In 1962 modern languages were added to the curriculum and a small language laboratory established. At the same time there was further enrichment in the form of courses in cultural anthropology, world religions, and international relations.

An interesting version of junior year abroad has enabled a group of 18 students led by a faculty husband-and-wife team to spend the academic year 1965–1966 studying at the University of Edinburgh in Scotland.

University of Wisconsin-Milwaukee

One of the most urgent and frequently ignored aspects of international educational exchange has been the exchange of those who are themselves professionally involved in education. The proportion of teachers and future teachers travelling abroad for an educational experience has been small. This is particularly true of those Americans involved in education although somewhat less true of those involved in education in foreign, particularly developing, countries.

The School of Education of the University of Wisconsin-Milwaukee is one of an increasing number of schools deliberately setting about to expend programs in the field of international education. The type of program they are offering allows unparalleled experience to their faculties of education by giving them an opportunity to be exposed to the problems of another culture and possible solution. At the same time, the teachers and future teachers within a foreign country are given opportunity of deepening and broadening their knowledge—in this way they can contribute vitally and materially to the establishment of an educational system in their own country. Few things are more important—to developing countries in particular—as the improvement and expansion of their own educational system. The effect on the economic, social and political life of the country is enormous.

The University of Wisconsin-Milwaukee is a relatively young school. Nevertheless in 1965, the School of Education had begun its fourth year of a training program on the Milwaukee campus for 42 educators coming from high schools in Venezuela. In order to drastically reform the secondary education system in Venezuela, this program, in cooperation with the Agency for International Development and the Ministry of Education of Venezuela, sends groups of Venezuelan educators to the University of Wisconsin in Milwaukee for a year of study, language training and school internships. Fifty per cent of the group concentrate on vocational education while the others focus on secondary education.

In addition, the School of Education set up a program for 30 educators from the Ministry of Education. Sponsored jointly with the Ministry of Education of Venezuela and the Agency for International Development, this program is geared to education in specialized areas at the level of the master's degree. Participants receive

(1) intensified English instruction, (2) graduate study in the fields of educational research, and (3) in-service education and extended internship opportunities.

A third component the University of Wisconsin-Milwaukee has in the development of Venezuelan education involves faculty members of the School of Education in Milwaukee who are working under the supervision of the Venezuelan Ministry of Education and its Educational Planning Commission. Three pilot schools already are the focus of their efforts and others will be designated in the near future.

In order to guarantee quality in their efforts, the School of Education has limited its efforts in the field of education to Latin America. Besides its relationships with education in Venezuela, it has developed programs in Colombia and Brazil.

In Colombia, its program is handled through the University of Antioquia. It involves not only translation, adaptation and exchange of professional materials but also undertakes another educational endeavor: the education of three Colombian professors as graduate students during a year spent at the University of Wisconsin in Milwaukee, and the education of a fourth in an advanced program so that he can take over a supervisory position when he returns to Colombia. Moreover, the services of a faculty from Milwaukee are given to the School of Education at Antioquia University. In addition to regular correspondence with former students, the University of Wisconsin-Milwaukee is planning a training project in secondary education similar to its comprehensive program in Venezuela.

In Brazil, the School of Education is active in training Brazilian educators on its Milwaukee campus. The School of Education works with Escola Johnson, an experimental elementary school in Fortaliza, Ceara, Brazil sponsored by The Johnson Foundation. Faculty of the School of Education in Milwaukee have visited Escola Johnson in a consultive capacity. The staff of Escola Johnson have studied at the University of Wisconsin-Milwaukee where they selected and translated educational materials to be used in Brazil.

Four Brazilian educators studied educational administration at the University of Wisconsin-Milwaukee under the auspices of the United States Office of Education. In addition to special English training, this group of educators enroll in regular academic courses both for credit and audit. They have an active schedule of field observation and internships.

There are a number of other programs at the School of Education on the Milwaukee campus which are part of its international education effort. The staff of the Milwaukee school and faculty of the University of Puerto Rico exchange places each summer. Also in the summer, the School of Education conducts a two week post summer session seminar for foreign students at colleges and universities throughout the United States. In the past, these sessions, held in cooperation with the United States Office of Education, have focused on forces which affect change both in education and on a democratic society.

Other programs of the United States government have their effect on the International Education program of the University of Wisconsin-Milwaukee. Groups of visiting educators occasionally spend two or three months on the campus for special study. While there, they engage in school visitations and other specially designed activities as part of a program of special study—or non-degree-programs. The Peace Corps has had an unusual impact on the university. It is one of four major training centers for Peace Corps volunteers in the United States. As such, its training programs for volunteers going to Latin America have complemented the efforts of the School of Education in Latin American education. In addition, graduate assistantships in education have been awarded to returning Peace Corps volunteers; these returning volunteers have worked in the campus elementary school, on the Latin American Project, on science education and on other educational endeavors.

In the future, the University of Wisconsin plans to expand its efforts in international education in order to meet the increasing demand for such programs. In 1966 it is handling a study tour of Venezuelan leaders in primary education and is making a survey to assess what the educational operations and facilities are in Venezuela. This is being done in cooperation with the Ministry of Education and The Ford Foundation. The purpose: to plan a long range strategy design for Venezuelan education. Another future proposal may result in the establishment of a program leading to the master of science degree in international education.

It is interesting to observe that since 1962 the staff of the programs in international education on the Milwaukee campus has grown from three to twenty-two full time and thirteen part-time members. There are fourteen full-time faculty members in Venezuela, as one to two year resident consultants. Latin American educators who have completed programs with the University of Wisconsin-Milwaukee have assumed vital positions in the Venezuelan educational system. The efforts of this growing Milwaukee campus in Latin America education have had a significant effect on both the campus in Milwaukee and on the educational system in Latin America—and this in a relatively short time. The need for such programs is great.

Other Colleges and Universities in the United States

The growing international dimension of the programs of the State University of New York deserves highlighting. In January, 1966, a new program of International Studies and World Affairs was established. Its headquarters, the International Center at Planting Fields, New York, will coordinate and direct the international programs of all of the university's fifty-seven campuses. The Institute for American Studies and Life at Planting Fields will enroll foreign students and teachers, while the Institute for Developing Nations will direct technical and educational assistance programs. This bold coordination of the international activities of a sprawling state university system will surely influence planning in other state educational networks as they meet similar problems.

Several colleges and universities have initiated programs for American students to work in developing nations. The opportunity for the student is a concrete and challenging experience. In addition, it offers the developing country a service under terms respectful of their sovereignty. The University of New Mexico accepts individuals with an M.A. (although a Ed.D. or Ph.D. is preferred) and with experience in the problems of educational development abroad into an eighteen month program of experience working in the national ministry of education, or in the regional or international planning offices of Latin American countries. This program is a good example of an unfortunately rare but highly valuable experience for educators in the United States.

The Sloan School of Management of Massachusetts Institute of Technology has a similar program for American students to work in African ministries after two years of post-graduate work at the MIT School of Industrial Management, Harvard Business School, or either the Harvard or Yale Law Schools.[10] This is yet another imaginative program answering the need of the American student for significant working experience abroad and the even more crying need of the developing countries for crucial and rare skills available only in trained personnel.

Schools Abroad

There are a number of opportunities to study and teach abroad in American-sponsored schools, in institutes for foreigners, in the colleges and universities of many countries abroad. This avenue should not be left unexplored. Many European colleges and universities will accept Americans at the graduate level. Special institutes such as the Salzburg seminar in Austria enroll a selected number of Americans. American-sponsored schools are especially apt to hire American teachers.

The American University of Beirut (AUB)

Because it is the most important, and largest, American university abroad, and is becoming a great international center of learning, the American University of Beirut deserves special attention. It presents rather unusual opportunities both to students and faculty seeking an international educational experience.

Celebrating its one hundredth anniversary in 1966–1967, AUB, as it is usually called, serves over 3,000 students from 60 countries. The majority of students are from the Arab countries, with Lebanon itself quite naturally providing the largest student contingent.

AUB has been called "an international university with an American flavor," for, though Arab studies (language, literature, and history) are an important part of the curriculum, the University is patterned after American institutions, and the language of instruction since 1880 has been English. AUB has an outstanding medical school, a college of arts and sciences, as well as engineering and agricultural schools. The campus is located on a rocky headland

---

[10] The unusual experiences of these students in the employ of African governments are related in an interesting article "Fifty-two People on a Continent," John McPhee, *The New Yorker,* March 5, 1966, pp. 101–150.

(Ras Beirut) and is backdropped by the high Lebanon range with its lovely villages and mountain resorts.

Information about opportunities to study at AUB can be obtained directly from the Registrar. There are numerous scholarships, most of which are provided by the United States government for students from other countries. There are also more limited opportunities for Americans, as instructors from the United States, either on one to two year exchange professorships or three year contracts.

The American Community School, the International College (a preparatory school for AUB) and other schools are also located in Beirut. These institutions generally have openings for qualified faculty, especially from the United States, but also have openings for instructors from other countries.

Cooperative Arrangements

To surmount the obstacles of limited resources which beset so many American institutions of higher learning, utilizing the cooperative arrangements that exist between a number of American colleges and universities is a practical and commendable solution. There is a growing realization of the values of inter-institutional cooperation in large universities and small colleges alike. Particularly in international education, where costs and risks are high, this is a good solution.

The Associated Colleges of the Midwest sponsor a number of programs for academic year, summer study, and research programs at selected centers abroad. The Inter-University Committee on Travel Grants for Study and Research in Bulgaria, Czechoslovakia, Hungary and the Soviet Union is precisely what its title implies. The Great Lakes Colleges Association emphasizes non-Western studies through fellowships for faculty and students in Japan, Yugoslavia, and Colombia.

Comprehensive information about other cooperative arrangements can be found in *Undergraduate Study Abroad*.[11]

There are many guides to the programs of the American colleges and universities for study abroad. The most authoritative is *Under-*

---

[11] Institute for International Education, *Undergraduate Study Abroad,* Report of the Consultative Service on U.S. Undergraduate Study Abroad (New York: The Institute, 1964).

graduate Study Abroad. Very helpful is *Intercultural Education.*[12] For foreign students wishing to study in the United States the most helpful publications are those of the Institute for International Education, particularly its *Handbook of International Study: for Foreign Nationals.*[13] The best statistical overview is their annual publication, *Open Doors.*

[12] Education and World Affairs, *International Education* (New York, 1965).

[13] Institute for International Education, *Handbook of International Study: For Foreign Nationals* (New York: The Institute, 1965).

CHAPTER VI

Conclusion

A brief history of cultural exchange and its evolution into what is known today as international educational exchange may have helped illuminate the background and put into perspective the discussion of the role of international organizations, national government and its various agencies, the educational institutions, both public and private, the patterns and forms of international exchange programs, and the prime opportunities which exist for those seeking this kind of educational experience. Hopefully, this book offers many clues to help achieve a successful experience.

"International education" has many meanings. In the past, it was piecemeal and unplanned.[1] Stretching through that past are the many historical strands which have been converging—here in the United States in the post-war period—into two major strands, closely interwoven. One strand is that of international education *per se*. Specifically, this entails conscious reform and regrouping of the educational system so as to incorporate learning about the contemporary world. Thus this takes form when curriculums incorporate world affairs and international understanding as an integral part of learning and when the related form of international educational exchange becomes a built-in part of the educational system.

The other strand is "the new and noble adventure" which the President of the United States has outlined as a coordinated and creative effort of government, thus making international education a primary part of the foreign policy of the United States.

The heart of the matter lies in the truly international aspect of the movement. As President Johnson said, "International education cannot be the work of one country. It is the responsibility and promise of all nations. It calls for free exchange and full collaboration.

[1] Education and World Affairs, *International Education Program, 1966* (New York: 1966), p. 5.

We expect to receive as much as we give, to learn as well as to teach."[2]

Earlier, Mr. Johnson had said, "In my own life, I have had cause again and again to bless the chance events which started me as a teacher."[3] To all who believe in the necessity for and the crucial role of international education, the positive concern of the Administration as well as the actions taken by the President to strengthen its role in the educational system and in government policy, bring the greatest encouragement.

The appointment of John Gardner, formerly President of the Carnegie Corporation, as Secretary of Health, Education, and Welfare, and the appointment of Charles Frankel, as Assistant Secretary for Cultural Affairs, following the publication of his book on American educational and cultural policy abroad, have been significant steps leading to the President's proposals for an International Education and Health Act of 1966. (These two men, among others, helped to prepare this bill.)

The most important feature of the President's program was that of establishing a Center for Educational Cooperation whose concern centered on the inherent purposes and values of international education:

> A further and profound significance of the Center is that it breaks down, at last, the artificiality with which we have divided at the ocean's edge our government's activities in this field. An elemental truth about international education is that it is composed of two inseparable parts: what goes on at home—the domestic programs of schools, colleges and universities, the "raising up" of new generations better educated about world affairs; and what goes on abroad—as American teachers, scholars, students, and institutions work cooperatively with their counterparts in other countries, learning much in the process and assisting them in their own further development.[4]

---

[2] President Lyndon B. Johnson in his Message on International Education, February 2, 1966. Text reprinted in *International Education Program, 1966*, pp. 22–31.

[3] President Johnson in his Smithsonian Address, September 16, 1965, *International Education Program, 1966*, pp. 18–21.

[4] *International Education Program, 1966*, p. 13.

Problems and Needs

Despite the glow of achievement which surrounds international education as a result of the Administration's actions, some problems remain. These were outlined in an appraisal by the staff of Education and World Affairs in March, 1966. These are problems which should be tackled at once. The manpower shortage is one, as the need is urgent for staffing positions in international education both here and abroad. There is need for closer bi-national collaboration in planning major international programs. The "foreign student problem" in the United States still exists, especially in terms of evaluation, screening, and admission to United States institutions. The Fulbright Program after twenty years needs a thorough over-hauling, and the whole apparatus of governmental and quasi-governmental boards and bodies must be reviewed in light of changed and changing conditions.[5]

Some sort of a tool is needed to facilitate the selection and admission of foreign students to American universities and colleges. Such a service is needed both by the universities, who are deluged by applications from abroad, and by the foreign student, who is overwhelmed by the numbers of colleges and universities in the United States and who needs help in distinguishing among them.

Education and World Affairs has recently published a report of a committee which was appointed to make recommendations about procedures that can be set up to meet problems confronting those involved with enrolling students from abroad in the United States. This good report published as *The Overseas Selection of Foreign Students* makes a number of cogent suggestions. It summarizes well the scope of the problem and the dimensions of its solution.

At the present time, a number of private organizations have established overseas offices in order to improve their services to foreign students. At the same time, the government of the United States has individuals in all of its overseas posts who are either directly or indirectly concerned with the selection of foreign nationals for education in the United States. The aforementioned report has high praise for the services of the Institute of International Education in its overseas offices, and for those of the Amer-

---

[5] *Ibid.*, p. 16.

ican Friends of the Middle East. It praises, in particular, the valuable and pioneering screening and selection techniques used by the African Scholarship program of American Universities of the African-American Institute which would be impossible without overseas offices. Of similar merit are the Foreign Student Screening Project of the American Economic Association and the program of Williams College. Williams has a center for the newly developing countries where courses in the study of economics has trained a highly selected group of young students who have since returned home and made valuable contributions to their own countries' economic development.

The volume of applications for places in American universities and colleges, particularly from students from the developing countries in Africa, Asia and Latin America, will continue to increase rapidly in the next decade. And the present facilities of public and private organizations, although highly commendable, are not adequate to handle the selection and testing of such increasing numbers. According to the report, a system must be devised in the face of these increasing numbers which will screen their applications and give them counseling and testing to meet the need and be fair to the students, the colleges and the universities.

First the dimensions of this need must be studied. The forces leading to the probable expansion of foreign student enrollment in the United States must be examined and an estimate of the size of this future demand of foreign students for an American education must be made. This estimate should be made for 1970–1975 and the numbers of possible applicants on the undergraduate and on the graduate levels must be distinguished. Both the advantages and the disadvantages to education in the United States as a result of increases in the number of foreign students in its institutions must be assessed. Finally goals must be established for the numbers of foreign students to be admitted to study in colleges and universities in the United States. Because the presently existing private and public organizations cannot be expected to handle the volume of work, that could be done better overseas, for students wishing to come to the United States, Education and World Affairs recommends that centers be established overseas for this specific purpose. The committee terms them Counseling, Evaluation, and Testing Centers. It suggests that they be established under the aegis of a Center for

Educational Cooperation in the United States under the jurisdiction of the Department of Health, Education, and Welfare. This government body is the same as that recommended by President Johnson in his proposals for an International Health and Education Act of 1966, and by John Gardner in his study of the Agency for International Development. Realistically, the report of Education and World Affairs suggests that a pilot center be set up in India. This site was chosen because of the need existing in India at the present time and also because of their existing progressive and rather large scale efforts to screen and evaluate applications in India. The report goes into considerable detail in its discussion of the functions and staffing of these Counseling, Evaluation, and Testing Centers. It recommends that the Philippines, in Africa, perhaps Nigeria, and in Latin America, perhaps Brazil, be given high priority.

In order that these overseas centers meet success, universities and colleges in the United States must cooperate. They must use the services offered, help staff them, make at least partial financial contribution, possibly on the basis of number of foreign students received through the services of the center.

The proposals made by Education and World Affairs are another of a series designed to hurdle the obstacles that both distance and a differing culture present to those wishing to study abroad. Its purpose is to overcome lack of information by establishing a middleman, the overseas office, who traffics in that vital commodity—information. The National Association of Foreign Student Affairs is another private organization deeply concerned with the need for overseas offices. This report effectively serves a useful purpose by presenting some of the pressing needs that exist in the field of international educational exchange.

In preceding chapters, the major programs for international exchange have been discussed and the major sources of information and of support in the form of grants have been outlined. It remains to pass along advice drawn from the experience of experts who either have done research in the field of international exchange or who are knowledgeable practitioners in the field of education.

For those who seek to enjoy an international educational experience, advice is free, easily tapped, and usually reliable. It is by no means limited to books and pamphlets. Every United States campus has its advisers; every agency of government, even remotely involved with international exchange, has its information experts often both here and in overseas countries. Especially for the student abroad who seeks an exchange opportunity in the United States, there are the advisers in American libraries, consulates, missions of the United States Information Service and the Agency for International Development, Binational Centers, and Fulbright Foundations in their countries. There are also the special services of the Institute of International Education in the United States and abroad, and the newer agencies with regional interests such as the African Scholarship Program of American Universities which are striving to help the qualified student find the right opportunity for study in the United States—appropriate for him and appropriate for the needs of his country.

There are many references in this text and in the bibliography at the end which will help the prospective exchangee find information on problems and pitfalls. Most of these references are concerned with the foreign student in the United States, though many of the findings apply as well to American students abroad.[6]

Taking a look at the less successful aspects of the international exchange program may help the prospective international student or instructor avoid situations which have led to unsuccessful experiences for others. For example, the Gardner report found that too many students coming to the United States were drawn from favored social and economic status groups, and it recommended that more grants be awarded to "have-nots" with talent. It suggested that the State Department Program seek out those who have "vigor and restlessness" for promoting desirable social and economic change. It recommended "field selection centers" abroad which would assist United States universities in their screening for good candidates and which would help the candidates themselves. Poor placement of foreign students has resulted all too often in frustration for student and university alike, so the report recommended that a special study

---

6 Robert D. Porter, ed., *Selected Studies in Inter-cultural Education* (New York: National Association for Foreign Student Affairs, 1962); Joseph A. Mestenhauser, ed., *Research in Programs for Foreign Students, A Report of the Waldenwoods Seminar* (New York: National Association of Foreign Student Advisors, 1961); United States Department of State, Bureau of Intelligence and Research, *Cross Cultural Education; A Bibliography of Government Sponsored and Private Research on Foreign Students and Trainees in the U.S. and Other Countries, 1946–64* (Washington, D.C.: U.S. Government Printing Office, 1965).

of private agencies be made to see whether placement could be improved.[7]

The Gardner report found need for more personal family contacts, and suggested that all State Department programs be geared to provide increased contacts and arrange for foreign students to meet a broader cross-section of American families. The poor quality of American professors and lecturers who went abroad was noted, and corrective measures in the form of increased salaries, support for dependents' travel, and increased use of direct recruitment were recommended.[8]

Since 1963, there have been improvements in all these areas, though it is often difficult for visiting professors from the United States to find travel funds for their families. Some still must go into debt to serve abroad, while some others have been able to save a substantial proportion of their salaries especially in cases where additional living allowances or stipends are provided. Salaries for full professors in some university projects abroad are fully the equivalent of salaries in the United States. The placement bureau called Overseas Educational Services, a part of Education and World Affairs, has helped overcome some of the problems of visiting professors going overseas. It has provided so much needed help in overcoming some of the problems of the exchange of teachers that further description of its services is appropriate here. The Overseas Educational Service was established in 1963 for the express purpose of expanding and improving the quality of the corps of American educators serving in colleges and universities in Africa, Asia and Latin America. It helps find appropriate posts abroad on behalf of American colleges and universities, disseminates information to individuals and institutions about teaching, particularly in developing countries, and helps recruit American faculty for such posts. It also helps solve personal, economic and career problems which evolve with extended service overseas. Before embarkation, it arranges orientation sessions for faculty and provides information on educational systems abroad. In the United States, it interviews and evaluates credentials of foreign graduate students who are candidates for academic positions in de-

---

[7] United States Advisory Commission on International Educational and Cultural Affairs, John W. Gardner, Chairman, *A Beacon of Hope—The Exchange of Persons Program* (Washington, D.C.: U.S. Government Printing Office, 1963).

[8] *Ibid.,* pp. 33–45.

veloping countries. As another dimension, the Overseas Educational Service supports research into the problems involved in overseas educational service by Americans.

All of these functions serve pressing needs. One example alone will illustrate the point: to staff the universities of Middle Africa through 1980 with adequate numbers of English-speaking faculty is going to require more than 5,000 educators.

A booklet, *Some Facts About Serving in Educational Posts Abroad* is published by the Overseas Educational Service. It summarizes some very important knowledge gained in the post-war years by the many American teachers who have served abroad. It lists the fields in which teacher demand is greatest, the qualifications necessary for applying for these unfilled positions, the variations in salary which exist between educational posts abroad, duration of service, and gives information about medical care, schools, and housing available.

In a few paragraphs the booklet states clearly the frustrations which American educators may face in overseas service. The advice of the Overseas Educational Service is that these obstacles must be faced realistically for:

> . . . they are not always overcome by high salaries. It may be the climate—too hot, too dry, too rainy or humid. It may be the inability to speak the local language. It may be lack of adequate schools for one's own children or lack of proper medical facilities.[9]

On the other hand, the American educator abroad most probably will find many pleasant surprises in store for him, such as a refreshing new set of friends and acquaintances, a chance to consider his specialty in a new context. Those most successful overseas, according to the Overseas Exchange Service, are those who are neither unduly depressed *or* exhilarated, but who, rather, carry to their work a strong sense of dedication. The Overseas Educational Service is quite right in pointing out that the potential for accomplishment in overseas education is very great. Since the need is greater overseas, the teacher can sense the worth of his or her own contribution.

One seeking overseas experience in university teaching should keep in mind that the Overseas Educational Service will accept applications, will maintain a register of those interested in either

---

9 *Some Facts About Serving in Educational Posts Abroad* (New York: Overseas Educational Service, n.d.), p. 5.

teaching, advising, administering or doing research abroad and will let the applicant know if an opportunity matching his predilections comes to its attention.

The "foreign student problem," referred to before, is really a series of problems extending beyond the selection and admissions apparatus. A more thoughtful and intelligent selection of foreign students would cure many of the problems which now arise. Some of these have been touched upon briefly in the text; others have not. A list of questions might be helpful to one who contemplates an educational experience in the United States.

It is obvious that there are students and students, problems and problems. To some extent "everyone has problems." Every student coming from abroad has his particular ones, just as every institution does. The following questions have been prepared as points of consideration; both students and institutions after "thinking through" the points may be helped in the direction of developing successful relationships abroad.

1. *Is it the right time for you to go abroad?* You may have no choice of time, but consider whether or not you are mature enough to leave your family and your own country. If you have a wife and children, consider what the effects will be upon them. Consider whether or not you have reached that proper stage in your education or career in your home country which will enable you to make the most of an opportunity to study abroad, whether that opportunity fits in with your career plans or not, if your study abroad will be helpful later on to your country. Are you seeking to go abroad just to get away from problems at home, for adventure, or for a real educational purpose? Should you plan to stay longer than one year?

2. *Can you afford to go abroad?* Looking ahead do you see adequate support over the entire period you will be studying abroad? For foreign students in the United States, uncertainty about the adequacy of their financial resources can become a harrowing problem.

3. *Are you prepared to study abroad?* Do you have adequate knowledge and skill in the language of instruction? If not, is there adequate opportunity to gain that knowledge before you go? Do you have some knowledge of the country where you plan to study or teach, if not, do you have adequate opportunity to gain this knowledge before you go? Do you know which are the best institutions abroad in your field of study or which institutions will give you ac-

ceptable preparation in your field? Can you gain admission to these schools? Are studies there acceptable in your own country?

By giving thoughtful answers to these questions a person can make his decision about going or not going. Decisions will come after consulting family, teachers, and colleagues. An expert in the field of international education can also be consulted—either in one's home country or through correspondence with advisers in institutions where one is thinking of applying.

Other Problems During Study Abroad

Language problems are the most frequent. "Credit" and "advancement" create special problems for nearly all students, foreign or not. For many foreign students the assessment for credit of work done in the home country can be a matter of dispute or, at least, of misunderstanding. Adjustment to new systems of examinations and of grading presents special problems. This has been a primary reason for establishing the special office of Foreign Student Advisers on many United States campuses.

Students and instructors who do not return to their home countries —where they often may be desperately needed—after completing their studies abroad pose a serious problem. This happens frequently among foreign nationals in the United States who face unsettled conditions at home. The Bureau of Social Science Research has a study in progress which shows that a large number of Koreans came to the United States to study over a specified period of time; they completed their studies but only a fraction have returned to Korea. In 1965, out of a total of 2,599 foreign students at the University of California at Berkeley, 597 either had taken up permanent residence or had asked for immigrant status.[10] In view of this situation, it seems that a question should be asked *before* allowing the experience abroad—as Cora DuBois put it in her 1956 study for the Carnegie Endowment—"Is the applicant firmly anchored in his home scene?"[11]

Another problem that has developed is the migratory foreign

[10] "Foreign Students, Berkeley," (Berkeley: University of California, December 28, 1965). Mimeographed.
[11] Cora DuBois, *Foreign Students and Higher Education in the United States* (Washington, D.C.: American Council on Education, 1962), p. 143.

student in the United States who starts proceedings immediately upon arrival to transfer from one educational institution to another. A fairly large number of inadequately-achieving foreign students, learning that they can secure easy admission to some of the lesser-known institutions in the United States, transfer quickly; some end up drifting from one school to another. Because of this, a Workshop on the Admission of Foreign Graduate Students (1964) passed this resolution:

> . . . that no United States graduate school should admit a student who had obtained his visa on an I–20 issued by another school unless the applicant had completed one year (or at least one semester) at that institution, be communicated to the Council of Graduate Schools, the Association of Graduate Schools, the various associations of graduate deans, the American Association of Collegiate Registrars and Admissions Officers, and other appropriate bodies.[12]

This, quoted in the Education and World Affairs report, is a brief but searching treatment of these sorts of problems, although the critique is directed mainly toward United States institutions rather than the visiting students.

The student from the United States.   So far, questions have centered mainly on the foreign student in the United States. Clearly many problems are similar and many of the same questions apply to students from the United States abroad. Specifically from the standpoint of the United States student and the United States institution, a few other questions and considerations are relevant.

Many of these problems were discussed during a conference of midwest deans on undergraduate study abroad, which was sponsored by the Institute for International Education and the Council on Student Travel, in cooperation with The Johnson Foundation, in March, 1966. Dr. Stephen Freeman, of Middlebury College, in summarizing their discussion, made the following points.

Why do students go abroad? Why do United States institutions send them abroad? Is the motivation the same? First, there are such broad reasons as general cultural enrichment, broadening of horizons, and extension of personality. These are thought of as "co-curricular" and are not for credit. Second, students go abroad for

---

[12] Education and World Affairs, *The Foreign Student: Whom Shall We Welcome?*, New York, 1964, pp. 19–20.

bona fide academic credit. The academic credit achieved abroad, however, is not likely to be considered equivalent to that achieved on the home campus. This can be a problem. Evaluation of credits earned abroad must be made with greater flexibility. Third, students and teachers go abroad for "specialized education," either languages, social studies, or both. A fourth motivation is "international understanding." This involves both a cultural impact on the individual and an impact upon national attitudes. If this motivation is too strong it may become an "ambassador complex," which has its dangers. The individual who goes primarily to be a good student usually is the best ambassador for his country.

Who should go? Should *all* United States students have the opportunity to study overseas? Should there be strict qualifications? Should they go singly or in groups? These are unanswered questions. In American institutions, programs range all the way from those of a small college, in which two or three students may go abroad alone for a year, to a college such as Kalamazoo College in Michigan which sends 90 per cent of all its students for an overseas experience. Most advisers believe that the group experience is usually better, and that the impact is greater upon the home college when they return.

At what level should the student go abroad? Sophomore year? Junior year? Post-graduate? What about the factors of personality and stamina? Studying abroad, especially in a foreign language, can be exhausting. There have been no investigations made on the relationship of personality or stamina to study abroad, although it goes without saying that an individual planning to study abroad should be a well-balanced and healthy person.

In choosing the locale for study abroad, American students and teachers tend to select the prestige universities in Western Europe. This is often a mistake. There are many better opportunities in non-university institutions abroad and many more profitable experiences to be gained in less prestigious places. There is also a better chance of mutuality in exchange with smaller institutions. For example, there are excellent teachers' colleges in Germany, called Pedagogical Institutes, which now participate in the German Academic Exchange Program. They have openings for American students and will welcome them. An educational experience in one of these institutions could be far more meaningful for many American students than a rather impersonal experience in one of the large German universities.

Language is a major problem for American students in foreign universities. Fluency is absolutely necessary in subject matter preparation. This is often difficult to achieve in some European university courses. One answer to this has been made by American colleges and universities which have set-up "islands" or special colleges abroad, organized, set up, and manned by the United States institution. A partially integrated plan or "peninsula" plan is an alternative in which a home curriculum is provided for students from the United States in an institution in a foreign country. Another solution to the language and adjustment problems is the summer home-stay with a family in the host country.

What about the cost? The year abroad usually turns out to be more expensive than anticipated, despite lower costs of tuition and somewhat lover living costs. Generalizations on cost are difficult to make, as much depends on the individual and the institutional arrangements. Additional costs for American students abroad usually turn out to be extras, such as the sightseeing trips and cultural events which students feel they cannot afford to miss while abroad.

For foreign students in the United States, financial problems loom large. Indeed, for most, an American education represents a very heavy financial sacrifice. The assistance provided by United States institutions is great, but it seems is never enough. Though it is considered highly undesirable, many students have to work part time, even during their first year.

What about the impact of study abroad? More research is needed. Despite the vastly increased interest in international education, too little is known about the results for the individual and the institution.

Among groups of American students there is often an observable let-down a few months after arrival abroad. The American dean should arrive at that crucial point to reassure them. What more has the individual gained by the experience? His problems are often exacerbated abroad. What does he bring back then? Educators must be certain that he brings back something more than would be the case if he stayed at home. This may mean more orientation before he goes.

A frequent criticism of United States students seeking an international experience is that they go for the fun of it and don't take seriously the formal educational part. The remark is "Tourism is not education." There is justification for this criticism, but college officers and faculty, aware of this pitfall, are not easily taken in by the individual who is simply going for a good time.

A peculiar problem posed by the student upon his return from overseas is called "decompression." Colleagues, instructors, and others describe the returning student with such phrases as "can't settle down" "makes all kinds of demands" "asks for special arrangements," "wants review of dormitory rules," "restless." This might be termed a reverse kind of cultural shock—adjusting back to the United States school or campus.

How do American students do when they return from abroad? A recent questionnaire asked a large cross-section of students "Do you feel you lost academically?" Ninety per cent answered "No." The experience abroad encourages independent study, as the American student rarely, if ever, finds the kind of spoon-feeding which he may receive on some American campuses.

In summary, the overseas experience should be integrated into the whole academic experience. The colleges in the United States should exercise greater flexibility in the granting of credit. They should allow for the increased opportunity for independent study, the greater impatience with old rules, and the indefinable but positive gain in maturity that is made by the individual who, getting away from his own society, can view it more objectively and begin to see it through the eyes of another culture.

A final word of advice to those who see support for study abroad: *plan ahead*. Applications are required a year in advance in most cases and failure to make them in time has led many an applicant to be disappointed.

This chapter has listed many problems of study abroad without even mentioning those personal problems of loneliness, of anxiety, of disappointment which are also a part of the experience.

All these problems should not be discouraging. No one is prepared in all ways. None of these warnings will stop those who are determined to qualify, for they will find ways to prepare themselves. They will go abroad, have an educational and personal experience which will enrich their entire career, their personal lives, and undoubtedly will affect the lives of those whom they love and those whom they teach.

Bon Echange!

Bibliography

Barber, H. Kenneth, ed., *AACTE Handbook of International Education Programs.* Washington, D.C. American Association of Colleges of Teacher Education, 1963.

Bereday, George Z. F., and Joseph A. Lauwerys, *The Yearbook of Education, 1964 Education and International Life.* London: Evans Brothers Limited, 1964.

Blum, Robert, *Cultural Affairs and Foreign Relations.* The American Assembly. Englewood Cliffs, N.J.: Prentice-Hall, Inc., 1963.

Board of Foreign Scholarships, *Exchange Scholars—A New Dimension in International Understanding, Third Annual Report,* Washington, D.C.: U.S. Government Printing Office, 1965.

————, *Teacher and Scholar Abroad, First Person Reports.* Washington, D.C.: U.S. Government Printing Office, 1964.

Brickman, William W., "International Education" in *Encyclopedia of Educational Research,* Walter S. Monroe, ed. New York: The Macmillan Company, 1950.

Bulletin on International Education, periodical of the American Council on Education.

"The Conference Board of Associated Research Councils in the United States —A Brief Historical Account with Special Reference to National and International Manpower Problems" *Social Science Information,* IV, June, 1965.

Coombs, Philip H., *The Fourth Dimension of Foreign Policy, Educational and Cultural Affairs.* Council on Foreign Relations. New York: Harper & Row, Publishers, 1964.

Council on Student Travel, *A Guide to Institutional Self-Study and Evaluation of Educational Programs Abroad,* New York, 1965.

————, *Semester and Academic Year Programs, Students Abroad,* New York, n.d.

Curti, Merle, *American Philanthropy Abroad, A History.* New Brunswick, N.J.: Rutgers University Press, 1963.

Davison, W. Phillips, *International Political Communication.* Council on Foreign Relations. New York: Frederick A. Praeger, 1965.

DuBois, Cora, *Foreign Students and Higher Education in the United States.* Washington, D.C.: American Council on Education, 1962.

Education and World Affairs, *AID and the Universities* by John Gardner. New York, 1964.

————, *Approaches to World Affairs at Six American Universities.* New York: Walker and Company, 1965.

————, *The College and World Affairs*. Report of the Committee on the College and World Affairs. New York, 1964.

————, *The Foreign Student: Whom Shall We Welcome?* New York, 1964.

————, *Intercultural Education*. An Information Service of Education and World Affairs, New York, 1965.

————, *International Education Program, 1966*. New York, 1966.

————, *The U.S. Office of Education: A New International Dimension*. New York, 1964.

Frankel, Charles, *The Neglected Aspect of Foreign Affairs, American Educational and Cultural Policy Abroad*. Washington, D.C.: Brookings Institution, 1965.

Fraser, Stewart, ed., *Government Policy and International Education*. New York: John Wiley & Son, Inc., 1965.

Foundation Library Center, *The Foundation Directory II Edition*. New York: Russell Sage Foundation, 1964.

Garraty, John A., and Walter Adams, *From Main Street to the Left Bank*. East Lansing: Michigan State University Press, 1959.

Higbee, Homer D., *The Status of Foreign Student Advising in United States Universities and Colleges*. East Lansing: Institute of Research on Overseas Programs, 1961.

Institute of International Education, *Annual Report, 1965*. New York, 1966.

————, *English Language and Orientation Programs in the United States*. New York, 1964.

————, *A Guide to the Admission and Placement of Foreign Students*. New York, 1962.

————, *Handbook on International Study: For Foreign Nationals* and *Handbook on International Study: For United States Nationals*. New York, 1965.

————, *Open Doors*. New York, 1965.

————, *Undergraduate Study Abroad*. Report of the Consultative Service on U.S. Undergraduate Study Abroad. New York, 1964.

International Educational and Cultural Exchange, quarterly of the United States Advisory Commission on International Educational and Cultural Affairs.

Johnson, Walter, and Francis J. Colligan, *The Fulbright Program, A History*. Chicago: University of Chicago Press, 1965.

Monroe, Walter S., ed., *Encyclopedia of Educational Research*. New York: The Macmillan Company, 1950.

National Association for Foreign Student Affairs, *Research in Programs for Foreign Students, A Report of the Waldenwoods Seminar,* Joseph A. Mestenhauser, ed., New York, 1961.

————, *Selected Studies in Inter-cultural Education,* Robert D. Porter, ed., New York, 1962.

Thomson, Charles A., and Walter H. C. Laves, *Cultural Relations and U.S. Foreign Policy*. Bloomington: Indiana University Press, 1963.

United National Educational, Social and Cultural Organization, *Study Abroad, 1964–1966,* New York, 1966.

United States Advisory Commission on International Educational and Cultural Affairs, *A Beacon of Hope—The Exchange of Persons Program.* Washington, D.C.: U.S. Government Printing Office, 1963.

——, *A Sequel to A Beacon of Hope—The Exchange of Persons Program.* Washington, D.C.: U.S. Government Printing Office, 1964.

United States Department of Health, Education and Welfare, *Teacher Exchange Opportunities and Summer Seminars.* Washington, D.C.: U.S. Government Printing Office, 1963.

United States Department of State, Agency for International Development, Contract Services Division, *AID-Financed Contracts as of June 30, 1965,* Washington, D.C.: U.S. Government Printing Office, 1965.

——, Bureau of Educational and Cultural Affairs, *Educational and Cultural Diplomacy, 1964.* Washington, D.C.: U.S. Government Printing Office, 1965.

——, Bureau of Educational and Cultural Affairs, *Educational and Cultural Exchange Opportunities.* Department of State Publication 7543, International Information and Cultural Series 83, April, 1965.

——, Bureau of Educational and Cultural Affairs, *Some U.S. Government Agencies Involved in International Activities.* Washington, D.C.: U.S. Government Printing Office, 1963.

——, Bureau of Intelligence and Research, *African Programs of U.S. Organizations, A Selective Directory.* Washington, D.C.: U.S. Government Printing Office, 1965.

——, Bureau of Intelligence and Research, *Cross Cultural Education: A Bibliography of Government Sponsored and Private Research on Foreign Students and Trainees in the U.S. and Other Countries, 1946–64.* Washington, D.C.: U.S. Government Printing Office, 1965.

——, Soviet and Eastern Europe Exchanges Staff, *Exchanges with the Soviet Union and Eastern Europe.* Washington, D.C.: semi-annual.

United States National Student Association, Educational Travel, Inc., *Work, Study, Travel Abroad, A Reference for Students.* New York: n.d.

The University and World Affairs. Report of the Committee on the University and World Affairs. New York: The Ford Foundation, 1961.

Wasson, Donald, ed., *American Agencies Interested in International Affairs.* Council on Foreign Relations. New York: Frederick A. Praeger, 1964.

Weidner, Edward W., *The World Role of Universities.* Carnegie Series in American Education. New York: McGraw-Hill Book Company, Inc., 1962.

Index